The Ignorant Schoolmaster

Five Lessons in Intellectual Emancipation

 Jacques Rancière

Translated, with an Introduction, by Kristin Ross

Stanford University Press
Stanford, California

Library of Congress Cataloging-in-Publication Data

Rancière Jacques.
  {Maître ignorant. English}
  The ignorant schoolmaster / Jacques Rancière ; translated, with
an introduction, by Kristin Ross.
      p.   cm.
  Translation of: Le maître ignorant.
  ISBN 0-8047-1874-1 (cl.)   :   ISBN 0-8047-1969-1 (pbk.)
    1. Jacotot, Jean-Joseph, 1770–1840.   2. Educators—
France—Biography.   3. Education—Philosophy.
4. Education—France—Parent participation.   I. Title.
LB675.J242R3613   .   1991
370'.1—dc20   90-26745
                                                         CIP

♾ This book is printed on acid-free paper.

Original printing 1991
Last figure below indicates year of this printing:
07   06   05   04   03   02   01   00   99

The Ignorant Schoolmaster

Five Lessons in
Intellectual Emancipation

Contents

Translator's Introduction

In *The Ignorant Schoolmaster* Jacques Rancière recounts the story of Joseph Jacotot, a schoolteacher driven into exile during the Restoration who allowed that experience to ferment into a method for showing illiterate parents how they themselves could teach their children how to read. That Jacotot's story might have something to do with the post-1968 debates about education in France was not immediately apparent to most of the book's readers when it appeared in 1987. How could the experiences of a man who had lived all the great pedagogical adventures of the French Revolution, whose own utopian teaching methods knew a brief—if worldwide and perfectly serious—flurry of attention before passing rapidly into the oblivion Rancière's book rescues them from—how could these experiences "communicate" with administrators face to face with the problems of educating immigrant North African children in Paris, or with intellectuals intent on mapping the French school system's continued reproduction of social inequalities? Rancière's book explained nothing about the failures of the school system;* it entered directly into none of the con-

---

*French journalism of the 1980's spoke frequently about "l'échec de l'école"; this failure was usually certified by comparing the percentage of French students who attain the *baccalauréat* (30 percent in 1985) with the percentage of high school graduates in Japan (75 percent) and the United States (85.6 percent). Given the advanced nature of the French *bac*—it includes something like two years of what Americans view as college-level work—these statistics perhaps

temporary polemical debates. Its polemics, dramatically recounted in the second half of the book, were rather those of the era of the ignorant schoolmaster, Joseph Jacotot: the effects of Jacotot's unusual method; its fate at the hands of the reformers and pedagogical institutions it undermined; its effacement by the educational policies put into effect, under the auspices of François Guizot and Victor Cousin, by the July Monarchy during the 1830's. The names of the most listened-to theoretical voices on post-'68 education—those of Pierre Bourdieu and Jean-Claude Milner—are not mentioned by Rancière. Yet the book's subject was obviously education. Key words like "lessons" and "intellectual," "ignorant" and "schoolmaster" appeared, if in a somewhat paradoxical arrangement, in its title. And education was again, in the 1980's, under scrutiny in France.

Readers in France had difficulty situating the book, as they have had difficulty, generally speaking, keeping up with the maverick intellectual itinerary of its author. For although in 1965, Rancière published *Lire le capital* with his teacher Louis Althusser, he was better known for his celebrated leftist critique of his coauthor, *La Leçon d'Althusser* (1974), and for the journal he founded the same year, *Révoltes logiques*. Trained as a philosopher, a professor of philosophy at the University of Paris, but immersed rather unfashionably since 1974 in early-nineteenth-century workers' archives, Rancière wrote books that eluded classification—books that gave voice to the wild journals of artisans, to the daydreams of anonymous thinkers, to worker-poets and philosophers who devised emancipatory systems alone, in the semi-unreal space/time of the scattered late-night moments their work schedules allowed them.[1] Were these books primarily history? The philosophy of history? The history of philosophy? Some readers took *Le Maître ignorant* to be a fragment of anecdotal history, a curiosity piece, an archival oddity.

---

indicate the elite nature of French schooling, its system of professional and vocational "tracking." From nearly a quarter to a third of working-class and rural students fail the preparatory course for the *bac*, against under 3 percent for those from professional families.

Educators read it—some quite anxiously, given Jacotot's affirmation that anyone can learn alone—in the imperative, as a contemporary prescriptive, a kind of suicidal pedagogical howto. A few reviewers read it on the level at which it might, I think, most immediately address an American or British readership only beginning to come to terms with the legacies of a decade of Reaganism and Thatcherism: as an essay, or perhaps a fable or parable, that enacts an extraordinary philosophical meditation on equality.

Bourdieu and the New Sociology

The singular history of each national collectivity plays a considerable role in the problems of education. Though the English translation appears in very different conditions,* it may be useful to begin by discussing the book's French context, a context still profoundly marked by the turbulence of the student uprisings of May '68 and by the confusions and disappointments, the reversals and desertions, of the decade that followed: the all but total collapse of the Parisian intelligentsia of the Left, the "end of politics" amid the triumph of sociology.

For it was perhaps as a reaction to the unexpectedness of the May uprisings that the 1970's favored the elaboration of a number of social seismologies and above all energized sociological reflection itself: the criticism of institutions and superstructures, of the multiform power of domination. In the wake of the political failure of '68, the social sciences awoke to the study of power: to the New Philosophers' self-promotional media takeover, to Michel Foucault, but most importantly, perhaps, to the sociology of Pierre Bourdieu—the enormous influence of whose work would, given the time lag and ideology of translation, begin in earnest in the English-speaking world only in the early 1980's. No less than the New Philosophers, Bourdieu

---

*In the United States today, for example, arguments about equality invariably turn on the subject of race—not surprisingly in the only major industrial nation built on a legacy of domestic slavery.

could be said to have profited from both the success and the failure of the May movement, the first granting his work the energy and posture of critique, the second reinforcing in it the gravitational pull of structure.

If Bourdieu's work had little serious impact on methodological debates among professional sociologists, its effect on historians, anthropologists, professors of French, educational reformers, art historians, ghetto high school teachers, and popular journalists was widespread. In the introduction to *L'Empire du sociologue* (1984), a collection of essays edited by Rancière and the *Révoltes logiques* collective, the authors attribute the extraordinary success of Bourdieu's themes of reproduction and distinction—the phenomenon of their being, so to speak, in everyone's head—to the simple fact that they *worked*, which is to say that they offered the most thorough philosophy of the social, the one that best explained to the most people the theoretical and political signification of the last twenty years of their lives. Bourdieu had produced, in other words, a discourse entirely in keeping with his time, a time that combined, in the words of the editors, "the orphaned fervor of denouncing the system with the disenchanted certitude of its perpetuity."[2]

Before May 1968, steeped in the theoretical and political atmosphere of the Althusserian battle for revolutionary science against ideology, Bourdieu and Jean-Claude Passeron published *Les Héritiers* (1964), an analysis of the University that helped fuel the denunciation of the institution by showing it to be entirely absorbed in the reproduction of unequal social structures. The post-May dissipation of hopes for social change, however, served only to amplify the influence of that work, and particularly of its theoretical sequels, *La Reproduction* (1970) and *La Distinction* (1979).[3] Bourdieu's structuralist rigor with a Marxist accent permitted an exhaustive interpretive analysis of class division and its inscription—minutely catalogued in the tiniest details of posture or daily behavior—an analysis that could carry on an existence entirely divorced from the practical hypotheses of Marxism or the naïvetés of hope for social transformation. It allowed, *Révoltes logiques* argued, "the denunciation of both the mechanisms of domination and the illusions of liberation."[4]

Rancière, in his own critical contribution to the volume, attacked Bourdieu and the new sociology as the latest and most influential form of a discourse deriving its authority from the presumed naïveté or ignorance of its objects of study: in the realm of education, the militant instructors in *La Reproduction* who need the legitimacy of the system's authority to denounce the arbitrariness of that legitimacy; and the working-class students excluded from the bourgeois system of favors and privileges, who do not (and cannot) understand their exclusion. By tracing the passage from *Les Héritiers* to *La Reproduction*, Rancière uncovered a logic whereby the social critic gains by showing democracy losing. It was, for example, all too obvious, he wrote, to say that working-class youth are almost entirely excluded from the university system, and that their cultural inferiority is a result of their economic inferiority. The sociologist attained the level of "science" by providing a tautology whose systemic workings, veiled to the agents trapped within its grip, were evident to him alone. The perfect circle, according to Rancière, was made "via two propositions":

1. Working-class youth are excluded from the University because they are unaware of the true reasons for which they are excluded (*Les Héritiers*).
2. Their ignorance of the true reasons for which they are excluded is a structural effect produced by the very existence of the system that excludes them (*La Reproduction*).[5]

The "Bourdieu effect" could be summed up in this perfect circle: "they are excluded because they don't know why they are excluded; and they don't know why they are excluded because they are excluded." Or better:

1. The system reproduces its existence because it goes unrecognized.

2. The system brings about, through the reproduction of its existence, an effect of misrecognition.[6]

By rehearsing this tautology, the sociologist placed himself "in the position of eternal denouncer of a system granted the ability to hide itself forever from its agents": not only did the sociologist see what teacher (and student) did not, he saw it *because* the teacher and student could not. Wasn't the ultimate concern evinced by the logic of the new sociology, Rancière suggested, that of reuniting its realm, legitimating its specificity as a science through a naturalizing objectification of the other?

Pedagogical Reforms

The sociological theories of Bourdieu and Passeron offered something for everyone. For the enlightened reader, the disabused Marxist, they offered the endlessly renewable pleasure of lucidity, the *frisson* of demystification and the unveiling of the clockwork mechanics of a functionalism usually reserved for the structuralist interpretation of fiction. But for the progressive educator they offered the justification for a series of attempts to reform the social inequities of the school system— and this especially after François Mitterand and the socialists were elected in 1981. At the level of governmental education policy, the Mitterand administration was riven by two warring ideological tendencies, embodied in the persons who successively occupied the position of Minister of Education, Alain Savary and Jean-Pierre Chevènement.

Savary, imbued with something of the spontaneous, libertarian ethos of May '68 and with the heady early moments of enacting the socialist agenda, saw his mission as that of reducing, through a series of reforms, the inequalities diagnosed by Bourdieu and Passeron. If petit-bourgeois instructors, intent on capitalizing on the distinctions conferred on them by their knowledge were, as Bourdieu and Passeron argued, complacently reproducing the cultural models that acted to select "inheritors" and legitimate the social inferiority of the dispossessed, then, Savary's reformers argued, a new educational community must be established: one based on undoing the rigid stratification of scholars and their knowledge—a kind of leveling at the top—and creating a convivial, open, egalitarian atmosphere in the schools, which would be attentive to the "whole personality" of the child. Savary, for instance, favored a compensatory attitude to unequal opportunity. He had "priority zones" designated that saw supplementary funding, extra teaching positions, and specially designed curricula established in elementary schools and high schools situated in poor neighborhoods.

When Savary's successor, Chevènement (currently Minister of Defense under Mitterand), came to power in 1984, he announced a halt to such attempts at egalitarian reform. Under the watchword of "republican elitism," Chevènement underscored the imperatives of technological modernization and competition for France in a period of worldwide economic crisis. Advocating a return to the Encyclopedist, rationalist, Enlightenment principles of Jules Ferry and the Third Republic, he called for the restoration of grammar, rigid examinations, civic instruction—a kind of curricular "back to basics," and a return to the rhetoric of selection that so long characterized French schooling. That a violent polemic concerning the values of education should erupt in the journalism of the mid-1980's—a moment of profound general anxiety about the question of French "identity" in the face of rising immigration—was not surprising. But the terms of the debate were all too familiar, as were the polarized positions that resulted: the more Rousseauist disciples of Savary arguing that even a "republican" elitism could lead only to the exclusion and marginalization of an important percentage of French youth; the "Enlightenment" followers of Chevènement arguing that a socialist education system must be rational and scientific.

In intellectual circles, the somewhat brutal transition from the warm bath of Savary to the science of Chevènement was facilitated by the publication in 1984 of the linguist Jean-Claude

Milner's controversial polemic, *De l'école*. (Milner appeared on
the popular French literary television show "Apostrophes" to
talk about his book and was invited by Chevènement to the
ministry to discuss his ideas on education.) Milner attributed
all the ills of the French system to a plot launched against
knowledge by a "triple alliance" of stingy administrators, hastily accredited parvenu high school teachers, and well-intended
reformers bent on advancing something they called "pedagogy"—what for Milner amounted to nothing more than the
empty science of teaching how to teach. These pseudo-
progressive advocates of the vaguely religious and virtuous vo-
cation of pedagogy produced, according to Milner, a purely par-
asitic discourse: reform after reform whose ends lay in sacrificing
true scholarly research and passion for a "convivial schoolroom
atmosphere." Not the least provocative of his assertions was
that a teacher did not have to like children to be a good teacher.
Hearkening back approvingly to the rigors of the Third Republic, he argued that schools and teachers should dispense
with modeling the "whole person" and view their task instead
simply and unequivocally as that of transmitting knowledge,
as "instructing," not "educating." The unequal relation between teacher and student was not to be dismantled but rather
celebrated, for in its inequality, as in that of psychoanalyst and
patient, lay the key to success. Inequality produced in the student the desire to know. True equality in schooling meant transmitting the same knowledge to each student.

In his review of Milner's book,[7] Rancière concurred with the
linguist's frank characterization of the reformist programs as
"obscurantist" in their assumption that the best way to reduce
inequalities in the realm of formally transmitted knowledge was
to cut back on knowledge itself; "racist" in their supposition
that the children of the working class—and especially of im-
migrants—should be provided with a less "abstract" or "cultural" curriculum; and "infantilizing" in their ideology of
school as a vast, vaguely maternal enterprise based on "nurtur-
ing." But the solution to all this was not, Rancière argued, a

return to some notion of pure, scientific transmission à la Jules Ferry, for such a thing had never existed. Wasn't schooling under the Third Republic tainted by, if not obsessed with, a hygienic project of moral formation? The terms of the debate—Rousseau vs. Ferry—were misleading. Equality might reside in teaching the same thing to everyone, but it was simply not true that every child in France now—or at any time in the past—had a right to participate in the community of knowledge. Similarly, Milner's notion of pure scholarly passion, Rancière suggested, masked the interests of the aristocrats of education, the mandarins at the top of the university and grant-funding hierarchies, whose concern lay in preserving, in the face of a rising tide of hastily accredited instructors, the traditional privileges of the possessors of culture.

The Lesson of Althusser

Milner and Rancière shared a student activist past, a friendship, a teacher—Louis Althusser—and a theoretical formation; twenty years previously, they had both belonged to the Union des Etudiants Communistes, the famous "cercle d'Ulm": the small group of young theorists including Etienne Balibar, Pierre Macheray, Jacques-Alain Miller, and Régis Debray, who attended Althusser's early seminars on Marx at the Ecole Normale. Rancière and Milner were among the signatories of the first—mimeographed—issue of the group's journal, the *Cahiers Marxistes-Leninistes*, an issue whose title, "The Function of Theoretical Formation," reveals its authors' early preoccupation with questions of education and the status of intellectual discourse.

A vast historical chasm separates Milner's *De l'école* from "The Function of Theoretical Formation"—a chasm filled with the momentous political defeat of European worker movements in France, Italy, Portugal, Greece, and Spain; the defeat of Althusserianism itself on the barricades of May; the Right's recuperation of May and its anarcho-libertarian ideology for the

Free Market; and the virtual suppression of historical materialism in France after 1975 at the hands of the intellectual currents of the New Philosophy and post-structuralism. And yet in certain of Milner's pronouncements about education, about questions of authority and equality, for instance, an echo of the old master's voice, that of Louis Althusser, can be heard: "The function of teaching," Althusser wrote in 1964, "is to transmit a determinate knowledge to subjects who do not possess this knowledge. The teaching situation thus rests on the absolute condition of *an inequality between a knowledge and a nonknowledge*."[8] For Milner, as for Althusser, the fundamental pedagogical relation is the one between knowledge and ignorance. The same historical chasm separates Rancière's *Le Maître ignorant* from his *La Leçon d'Althusser*, but Rancière's subject—education, or more broadly, the status of those who possess knowledge versus the status of those who don't—and orientation toward authority remain unchanged; both books, in fact, announce themselves as "lessons."

By writing *La Leçon d'Althusser*, Rancière performed what he called "the first clearing of the terrain" for the kind of reflection that has preoccupied him ever since: the consideration of the philosophical and historical relations between knowledge and the masses. Althusserianism, in *La Leçon d'Althusser*, emerges first and foremost as a theory of education. For Rancière, Althusser's only political—in the strict sense of the word—intervention occurred during the early moments of student unrest, when a controversy regarding higher education arose between the student union (UNEF) and the Communist Party. Student discontent had begun at that point to focus on the *forms* of the transmission of knowledge—the pedagogical relation of magisterial professors and docile students—as well as its ends: forming the future auxiliaries of the bourgeoisie. Already in the early 1960's, students had begun to question the arbitrariness of examinations and the ideology of individual research. In these early, tentative efforts—their slogan was "La Sorbonne aux étudiants"—politics appeared in a new form: in the questioning of

knowledge and its relation to political power and in the introduction of a new line of division among intellectuals between
the producers and the consumers of knowledge. Althusser's intervention was swift and clear. In an article entitled "Problèmes
étudiants" (1964), he outlined the correct priorities for Communist students. They must first develop their knowledge of
Marxism-Leninism and then conduct scientific analyses that
would yield objective knowledge of the University. What
should matter to Marxists was less the form—the pedagogical
relation in which knowledge was disseminated—than "the
quality of knowledge itself." Their task must be that of "discovering new scientific knowledge capable of illuminating and
criticizing the overwhelming illusions in which everyone is im-
prisoned," and the privileged vehicle for performing this task
was individual research. The real locus of class division in the
University was not in the inequitable relations between teachers
and students, but in the *content* of the teaching: "it is by the
very nature of the knowledge that it imparts to students that
the bourgeoisie exerts . . . the profoundest influence over
them."

For Rancière, the Althusserian concept of science—in fact,
the science/ideology distinction itself—had ultimately no other
function than that of justifying the pure being of knowledge,
and, more important, of justifying the eminent dignity of the
possessors of that knowledge. For if science (theory) forms an
enclave of freedom in a world of ideological enslavement, if science belongs to the intellectuals—the masters—and the critique of bourgeois content is reserved for those who already
know, then there is only one way for students to criticize their
masters' knowledge from the point of view of class, and that is
to become their peers. If everyone dwells in illusion (ideology),
then the solution can only come from a kind of muscular theoretical heroism on the part of the lone theorist. Rancière recounted what was for him the most graphic illustration of this:
Althusser's need to deny the antiauthoritarian May revolt as it
was happening in order to pretend later to "discover," through

chance and solitary research, and to propose as a risky hypothesis, what the mass student action had already revealed to everyone—the function of the school as an ideological apparatus of the state.[9]

Confronted with the events of May, the logic of Althusserianism reacts according to the predictable temporality of *the one who knows*. May '68 was not the *proper* moment. Empirical politics and theory must be dissociated from each other, and the position that enacted that dissociation was that of the educator—he who knows how to wait, how to guard his distance, how to take the time of theory. The last resource of philosophy is to eternalize the division of labor that grants it its place.[10]

The Practice of Equality

If the philosophical tradition is itself a product of the division between mental and manual labor, then what authority is to be granted the testimony of this tradition? And particularly when philosophy sets itself the task, as it delights in doing, of speaking for those whose presumed ignorance grants it its domain? Since *La Leçon d'Althusser*, Rancière's investigation of the origin, continuation, and occasional subversion of the hierarchical division of head and hand has been launched on two fronts. The first might be called the archival level, the documenting, chronicling, essentially recounting, of the experiences and voices of early-nineteenth-century workers who "transgressed the boundaries set for them": figures both marginal and central to workers' communities whose emancipation took the form of claiming for themselves what the middle classes assumed to be theirs alone, a realm of existence outside the one defined by the circle of material necessity. He focused on workers who claimed the right to aesthetic contemplation, the right to dead time—and, above all, the right to think. "I took the great *gauchiste* theme—the relations of intellectual and manual work—and put it in reverse: not the re-education of intellectuals, but the eruption of negativity, of *thinking*, into a social category always defined by the positivity of *doing*."[11]

This archival, narrative work has run parallel to—and entertains a crucial dialogue with—the second, more polemical and discursive front: Rancière's critique of the claims of bourgeois observers and intellectuals (philosophers, social historians, New Philosophers, sociologists) to know, and thus "speak for" or explicate, the privileged other of political modernity, the worker.[12]

Rancière's critique of the educational theories of Bourdieu, Althusser, and Milner shows them to have at least one thing in common: a lesson in inequality. Each, that is, by beginning with inequality, proves it, and by proving it, in the end, is obliged to rediscover it again and again.[13] Whether school is seen as the reproduction of inequality (Bourdieu) or as the potential instrument for the reduction of inequality (Savary), the effect is the same: that of erecting and maintaining the distance separating a future reconciliation from a present inequality, a knowledge in the offing from today's intellectual impoverishment—a distance discursively invented and reinvented so that it may never be abolished. The poor stay in their place. The same temporal and spatial distance separates the pedagogue from the student as separates the "explicator of the social" from the worker.

But what if equality, instead, were to provide the point of departure? What would it mean to make equality a *presupposition* rather than a goal, a *practice* rather than a reward situated firmly in some distant future so as to all the better explain its present infeasibility? This is the lesson provided by Joseph Jacotot's experience—*expérience* in the French Enlightenment sense of both "experiment" and "experience"—and the lesson whose political and philosophical timeliness Rancière affirms by recounting Jacotot's story.

All people are equally intelligent. This is Jacotot's startling (or naïve?) presupposition, his lesson in intellectual emancipation. And from this starting point (the result of an accidental discovery occasioned by the peculiar circumstances of exile), Jacotot came to realize that knowledge is not necessary to teaching, nor explication necessary to learning. "Explication," he writes, "is the myth of pedagogy." Rather than eliminating incapacity, explication, in fact, creates it. It does this in part by establishing the temporal structure of delay ("a little further along," "a little later," "a few more explanations and you'll see the light") that, writ large, would become the whole nineteenth-century myth of Progress: "the pedagogical fiction erected into the fiction of the whole society," and the general infantilization of the individuals who compose it. The pedagogical myth divides the world into two: the knowing and the ignorant, the mature and the unformed, the capable and the incapable. By the second half of *The Ignorant Schoolmaster*, the homology of delay that links the popular classes, the child, and the poor within the discourse of the republican "Men of Progress" surrounding Jacotot is all too clear.

The pedagogical fiction works by representing inequality in terms of velocity: as "slowness," "backwardness," "delay." Perhaps this homology of delay, the whole temporality of the "lag" that the book exposes, will provide the means for readers who have pondered the forms taken by the ideology of progress since Jacotot's time to trace the constellation (the term is Walter Benjamin's) that our own era forms with Jacotot's. For hasn't the pedagogical fiction of our own time been cast on a global scale? Never will the student catch up with the teacher; never will the "developing" nations catch up with the enlightened nations. Are even the critiques of "dependency theory" free of pedagogical rhetoric in their discussions of the Third World? To say this is to claim that a reading of *The Ignorant Schoolmaster* can suggest how today's much-heralded "democratization" of the globe— our own contemporary institutionalization and representation of progress—is just the new name for inequality.

In *The Ignorant Schoolmaster*, Rancière has found the means of illustrating and defending equality that extends to the very level of formal risks he has taken recounting the story. It is above all the book's formal procedures that have allowed Rancière to think the social itself in such a distinctly original fashion. For as Benjamin was not alone in realizing, "the concept of the historical progress of mankind cannot be sundered from the concept of its progression through a homogenous, empty time. And a critique of such a progression must be the basis of any criticism of the concept of progress itself."[14] The critique of progress, in other words, must intervene at the level of the progression, the speed or pacing, the practice of historical writing itself. Viewed from this perspective, the gradualist, "additive" notion of writing history—the slow, reasoned accumulation of data with which the historian fills an empty, homogenous time—begins to bear a distinct resemblance to the gradual, step-by-step acquisition of understanding through explication that Jacotot's method so dramatically explodes.*

If the historian's relation to the past—and to his or her readers—is not to be one of explication, then what can it be? Early writings of the *Révoltes logiques* collective announce its project to be that of creating an "alternative historical memory." This, I think, suggests a motivation akin to that of Benjamin's to blast, as he put it, "a unique experience of the past" out of the "continuum of history" for the purpose of wresting meaning from the past for the present. As the collective put it:

An episode from the past interests us only inasmuch as it becomes an episode of the present wherein our thoughts, actions, and strategies are decided. . . . What interests us is that ideas be events, that history be at all times a break, a rupture, to be interrogated only from the perspective of the here and now, and only politically.[15]

The motivation is clear. But what are the formal or rhetorical strategies, what are the writing practices, that allow an episode from the past to become an episode in the present? In the case of *The Ignorant Schoolmaster*, the story of Jacotot opens and ends

---

*Rancière is in fact best known in the United States among historians, for his polemical interventions concerning social history as a métier, and for his debates with particular social historians over the identity and consciousness of the artisan. See, especially, his exchange with William Sewell, Jr., and Christopher Johnson in "The Myth of the Artisan," *International Labor and Working Class History*, 24 (Fall 1983). See also what is the most thorough discussion of Rancière's relation to the practice of history, and of his work in general: Donald Reid's introduction to the translation of *La Nuit des prolétaires* (*Nights of Labor*; Philadelphia, 1989). Important essays by Rancière originally published in *Révoltes logiques* are available in *Voices of the People*, ed. Adrian Rifkin and Roger Thomas (London, 1988).

without Rancière doing, on one level, anything other than narrating it. Storytelling then, in and of itself, or *recounting*—one of the two basic operations of the intelligence according to Jacotot—emerges as one of the concrete acts or practices that verifies equality. (Equality, writes Jacotot, "is neither given nor claimed, it is practiced, it is *verified.*") The very act of storytelling, an act that presumes in its interlocutor an equality of intelligence rather than an inequality of knowledge, posits equality, just as the act of explication posits inequality.

But another, more unusual effect is created by the narrative style of the book: a particular kind of uncertainty that readers may experience concerning the identity of the book's narrator. The reader, in other words, is not quite sure where the voice of Jacotot stops and Rancière's begins. Rancière slips into Jacotot's text, winding around or worming in; his commentary contextualizes, rehearses, reiterates, dramatizes, elaborates, *continues* Jacotot; the effect is one of a complex echoing taking place between the author and Jacotot at the level of voice, as though an enormously sympathetic disciple of Jacotot's had, by some time-travel device familiar to readers of science fiction, turned up in the twentieth century. One existential grounding for such an echoing may be surmised. Jacotot's relation to post-Revolutionary France (his experiments, in a sense, *prolong* the revolutionary energies of 1789 into the France of the 1820's and 1830's) is doubled by Rancière's relation to 1968. The two are united by something like a shared lived relation to cycles of hope, then to cycles of discouragement, and on to the displacement of hope—a sequence that marks the experience of periods of revolutionary ferment and their aftermath. That such periods are also ones of productive ferment around the question of education—or *transmission*—goes without saying. But in the end it is emancipation—not education—that has drawn Rancière to Jacotot.

For the reader, this narrative uncertainty will prove productive, I think, for it has the effect of facilitating—creating the means for—the book's (nonexplicit, unexplicated) intervention into the present. Without explanation, the political timeliness of Jacotot's "naïveté" is affirmed. For Rancière, this particular book becomes the means by which his two previously separated activities—the archival, situated in the past, and the polemical, situated for the most part in the present of contemporary theory—are merged, a merging that in turn confounds any attempt to classify the book generically. Are the nineteenth-century republican Men of Progress, the founders of public education, the sociologists of today? And, if so, is the book a satire? Does a satirist's rage at the fallen reality of postmodernism, our own society of experts, drive the recitation of Jacotot's utopian experience? It is certainly clear, for example, that Rancière's (and Jacotot's) distinctive "untimeliness" stands in agonistic relation to the perfect timeliness and seamlessness of the "Bourdieu effect," the whole contemporary sociology of "systems of representation." Can Jacotot and his series of concrete practices verifying equality be marshaled to do battle with the dominant discourse of our own time, the discourse of a hidden truth and its demystification by the master explicator, the discourse that asserts that "there is no science but of the hidden"?[16]

The Ignorant Schoolmaster forces us to confront what any number of nihilistic, neo-liberal philosophies would have us avoid: the founding term of our political modernity, *equality*. And in the face of systematic attacks on the very idea, powerful ideologies that would relegate it to the dustbin of history or to some dimly radiant future, Rancière places equality—*virtually*—in the present. Against the seamless science of the hidden, Jacotot's story reminds us that equality turns on another, very different logic: in division rather than consensus, in a multiplicity of concrete acts and actual moments and situations, situations that erupt into the fiction of inegalitarian society without themselves becoming institutions. And in this, my rendering of the title of the book as *The Ignorant Schoolmaster* is perhaps misleading. For Jacotot had no school. Equality does not, as they say in French, "faire école."

The Ignorant Schoolmaster

Five Lessons in
Intellectual Emancipation

1   An Intellectual Adventure

In 1818, Joseph Jacotot, a lecturer in French literature at the University of Louvain, had an intellectual adventure.

A long and eventful career should have made him immune to surprises: he had celebrated his nineteenth birthday in 1789. He was at that time teaching rhetoric at Dijon and preparing for a career in law. In 1792, he served as an artilleryman in the Republican armies. Then, under the Convention, he worked successively as instructor for the Bureau of Gunpowder, secretary to the Minister of War, and substitute for the director of the Ecole Polytechnique. When he returned to Dijon, he taught analysis, ideology, ancient languages, pure mathematics, transcendent mathematics, and law. In March 1815, the esteem of his countrymen made him a deputy in spite of himself. The return of the Bourbons forced him into exile, and by the generosity of the King of the Netherlands he obtained a position as a professor at half-pay. Joseph Jacotot was acquainted with the laws of hospitality and counted on spending some calm days in Louvain.

Chance decided differently. The unassuming lecturer's lessons were, in fact, highly appreciated by his students. Among those who wanted to avail themselves of him were a good number of students who did not speak French; but Joseph Jacotot knew no Flemish. There was thus no language in which he could teach them what they sought from him. Yet he wanted to respond to their wishes. To do so, the minimal link of a *thing in common* had to be established between himself and them. At that time, a bilingual edition of *Télémaque* was being published in Brussels.* The thing in common had been found, and Telemachus made his way into the life of Joseph Jacotot. He had the book delivered to the students and asked them, through an interpreter, to learn the French text with the help of the translation. When they had made it through the first half of the book, he had them repeat what they had learned over and over, and then told them to read through the rest of the book until they could recite it. This was a fortunate solution, but it was also, on a small scale, a philosophical experiment in the style of the ones performed during the Age of Enlightenment. And Joseph Jacotot, in 1818, remained a man of the preceding century.

But the experiment exceeded his expectations. He asked the students who had prepared as instructed to write in French what they thought about what they had read:

He expected horrendous barbarisms, or maybe a complete inability to perform. How could these young people, deprived of explanation, understand and resolve the difficulties of a language entirely new to them? No matter! He had to find out where the route opened by chance had taken them, what had been the results of that desperate empiricism. And how surprised he was to discover that the students, left to themselves, managed this difficult step as well as many French could have done! Was wanting all that was necessary for doing? Were all men virtually capable of understanding what others had done and understood?[1]

Such was the revolution that this chance experiment unleashed in his mind. Until then, he had believed what all con-

---

*Fénelon's didactic and utopian 24-volume novel, *Télémaque* (1699), recounts the peregrinations of Telemachus, accompanied by his spiritual guide, Mentor, as he attempts to find his father, Odysseus. In it, Fénelon proposes an "Art of Reigning" and invents an ideal city, Salente, whose peace-loving citizens show exemplary civic virtue. The book was extremely displeasing to Louis XIV, who saw himself in the portrait of Idomeneus. But it was much admired by Enlightenment philosophers, who proclaimed Fénelon one of their most important precursors. In terms of Jacotot's adventure, the book could have been *Télémaque* or any other. —TRANS.

scientious professors believe: that the important business of the master is to transmit his knowledge to his students so as to bring them, by degrees, to his own level of expertise. Like all conscientious professors, he knew that teaching was not in the slightest about cramming students with knowledge and having them repeat it like parrots, but he knew equally well that students had to avoid the chance detours where minds still incapable of distinguishing the essential from the accessory, the principle from the consequence, get lost. In short, the essential act of the master was to *explicate*: to disengage the simple elements of learning, and to reconcile their simplicity in principle with the factual simplicity that characterizes young and ignorant minds. To teach was to transmit learning and form minds simultaneously, by leading those minds, according to an ordered progression, from the most simple to the most complex. By the reasoned appropriation of knowledge and the formation of judgment and taste, a student was thus elevated to as high a level as his social destination demanded, and he was in this way prepared to make the use of the knowledge appropriate to that destination: to teach, to litigate, or to govern for the lettered elite; to invent, design, or make instruments and machines for the new avant-garde now hopefully to be drawn from the elite of the common people; and, in the scientific careers, for the minds gifted with this particular genius, to make new discoveries. Undoubtedly the procedures of these men of science would diverge noticeably from the reasoned order of the pedagogues. But this was no grounds for an argument against that order. On the contrary, one must first acquire a solid and methodical foundation before the singularities of genius could take flight. *Post hoc, ergo propter hoc.*

This is how all conscientious professors reason. This was how Joseph Jacotot, in his thirty years at the job, had reasoned and acted. But now, by chance, a grain of sand had gotten into the machine. He had given no explanation to his "students" on the first elements of the language. He had not explained spelling or conjugations to them. They had looked for the French words that corresponded to words they knew and the reasons for their grammatical endings by themselves. They had learned to put them together to make, in turn, French sentences by themselves: sentences whose spelling and grammar became more and more exact as they progressed through the book; but, above all, sentences of writers and not of schoolchildren. Were the schoolmaster's explications therefore superfluous? Or, if they weren't, to whom and for what were they useful?

The Explicative Order

Thus, in the mind of Joseph Jacotot, a sudden illumination brutally highlighted what is blindly taken for granted in any system of teaching: the necessity of explication. And yet why shouldn't it be taken for granted? No one truly knows anything other than what he has understood. And for comprehension to take place, one has to be given an explication, the words of the master must shatter the silence of the taught material.

And yet that logic is not without certain obscurities. Consider, for example, a book in the hands of a student. The book is made up of a series of reasonings designed to make a student understand some material. But now the schoolmaster opens his mouth to explain the book. He makes a series of reasonings in order to explain the series of reasonings that constitute the book. But why should the book need such help? Instead of paying for an explicator, couldn't a father simply give the book to his son and the child understand directly the reasonings of the book? And if he doesn't understand them, why would he be any more likely to understand the reasonings that would explain to him what he hasn't understood? Are those reasonings of a different nature? And if so, wouldn't it be necessary to explain the way in which to understand them?

So the logic of explication calls for the principle of a regression ad infinitum: there is no reason for the redoubling of reasonings ever to stop. What brings an end to the regression and gives the system its foundation is simply that the explicator is the sole judge of the point when the explication is itself explicated. He is the sole judge of that, in itself, dizzying question:

has the student understood the reasonings that teach him to understand the reasonings? This is what the master has over the father: how could the father be certain that the child has understood the book's reasonings? What is missing for the father, what will always be missing in the trio he forms with the child and the book, is the singular art of the explicator: the art of *distance*. The master's secret is to know how to recognize the distance between the taught material and the person being instructed, the distance also between learning and understanding. The explicator sets up and abolishes this distance—deploys it and reabsorbs it in the fullness of his speech.

This privileged status of speech does not suppress the regression ad infinitum without instituting a paradoxical hierarchy. In the explicative order, in fact, an oral explication is usually necessary to explicate the written explication. This presupposes that reasonings are clearer, are better imprinted on the mind of the student, when they are conveyed by the speech of the master, which dissipates in an instant, than when conveyed by the book, where they are inscribed forever in indelible characters. How can we understand this paradoxical privilege of speech over writing, of hearing over sight? What relationship thus exists between the power of speech and the power of the master?

This paradox immediately gives rise to another: the *words* the child learns best, those whose meaning he best fathoms, those he best makes his own through his own usage, are those he learns without a master explicator, well before any master explicator. According to the unequal returns of various intellectual apprenticeships, what all human children learn best is what no master can explain: the mother tongue. We speak to them and we speak around them. They hear and retain, imitate and repeat, make mistakes and correct themselves, succeed by chance and begin again methodically, and, at too young an age for explicators to begin instructing them, they are almost all—regardless of gender, social condition, and skin color—able to understand and speak the language of their parents.

And only now does this child who learned to speak through his own intelligence and through instructors who did not explain language to him—only now does his instruction, properly speaking, begin. Now everything happens as though he could no longer learn with ᵗhe aid of the same intelligence he has used up until now, as though the autonomous relationship between apprenticeship and verification were, from this point on, alien to him. Between one and the other an opacity has now set in. It concerns *understanding*, and this word alone throws a veil over everything: understanding is what the child cannot do without the explanations of a master—later, of as many masters as there are materials to understand, all presented in a certain progressive order. Not to mention the strange circumstance that since the era of progress began, these explications have not ceased being perfected in order better to explicate, to make more comprehensible, the better to learn to learn—without any discernible corresponding perfection of the said comprehension. Instead, a growing complaint begins to be heard: the explicative system is losing effectiveness. This, of course, necessitates reworking the explications yet again to make them easier to understand by those who are failing to take them in.

The revelation that came to Joseph Jacotot amounts to this: the logic of the explicative system had to be overturned. Explication is not necessary to remedy an incapacity to understand. On the contrary, that very incapacity provides the structuring fiction of the explicative conception of the world. It is the explicator who needs the incapable and not the other way around; it is he who constitutes the incapable as such. To explain something to someone is first of all to show him he cannot understand it by himself. Before being the act of the pedagogue, explication is the myth of pedagogy, the parable of a world divided into knowing minds and ignorant ones, ripe minds and immature ones, the capable and the incapable, the intelligent and the stupid. The explicator's special trick consists of this double inaugural gesture. On the one hand, he decrees the absolute beginning: it is only now that the act of learning will begin. On the other, having thrown a veil of ignorance over everything that is to be learned, he appoints himself to the task of lifting it. Until he came along, the child has been groping blindly, figuring out riddles. Now he will learn. He heard words and repeated them. But now it is time to read, and he will not understand words if he doesn't understand syllables, and he won't understand syllables if he doesn't understand letters that neither the book nor his parents can make him understand—only the master's word. The pedagogical myth, we said, divides the world into two. More precisely, it divides intelligence into two. It says that there is an inferior intelligence and a superior one. The former registers perceptions by chance, retains them, interprets and repeats them empirically, within the closed circle of habit and need. This is the intelligence of the young child and the common man. The superior intelligence knows things by reason, proceeds by method, from the simple to the complex, from the part to the whole. It is this intelligence that allows the master to transmit his knowledge by adapting it to the intellectual capacities of the student and allows him to verify that the student has satisfactorily understood what he learned. Such is the principle of explication. From this point on, for Jacotot, such will be the principle of *enforced stultification.**

To understand this we must rid ourselves of received images. The stultifier is not an aged obtuse master who crams his students' skulls full of poorly digested knowledge, or a malignant character mouthing half-truths in order to shore up his power and the social order. On the contrary, he is all the more efficacious because he is knowledgeable, enlightened, and of good faith. The more he knows, the more evident to him is the distance between his knowledge and the ignorance of the ignorant ones. The more he is enlightened, the more evident he finds the difference between groping blindly and searching methodically, the more he will insist on substituting the spirit for the letter, the clarity of explications for the authority of the book. Above

---

*In the absence of a precise English equivalent for the French term *abrutir* (to render stupid, to treat like a brute), I've translated it as "stultify." Stultify carries the connotations of numbing and deadening better than the word "stupefy," which implies a sense of wonderment or amazement absent in the French.—TRANS.

all, he will say, the student must understand, and for that we must explain even better. Such is the concern of the enlightened pedagogue: does the little one understand? He doesn't understand. I will find new ways to explain it to him, ways more rigorous in principle, more attractive in form—and I will verify that he has understood.

A noble concern. Unfortunately, it is just this little word, this slogan of the enlightened—understand—that causes all the trouble. It is this word that brings a halt to the movement of reason, that destroys its confidence in itself, that distracts it by breaking the world of intelligence into two, by installing the division between the groping animal and the learned little man, between common sense and science. From the moment this slogan of duality is pronounced, all the perfecting of the ways of *making understood*, that great preoccupation of men of methods and progressives, is progress toward stultification. The child who recites under the threat of the rod obeys the rod and that's all: he will apply his intelligence to something else. But the child who is *explained to* will devote his intelligence to the work of grieving: to understanding, that is to say, to understanding that he doesn't understand unless he is explained to. He is no longer submitting to the rod, but rather to a hierarchical world of intelligence. For the rest, like the other child, he doesn't have to worry: if the solution to the problem is too difficult to pursue, he will have enough intelligence to open his eyes wide. The master is vigilant and patient. He will see that the child isn't following him; he will put him back on track by explaining things again. And thus the child acquires a new intelligence, that of the master's explications. Later he can be an explicator in turn. He possesses the equipment. But he will perfect it: he will be a man of progress.

Chance and Will

So goes the world of the explicated explicators. So would it have gone for Professor Jacotot if chance hadn't put him in the presence of a *fact*. And Joseph Jacotot believed that all reasoning should be based on facts and cede place to them. We shouldn't conclude from this that he was a materialist. On the contrary, like Descartes, who proved movement by walking, but also like his very royalist and very religious contemporary Maine de Biran, he considered the fact of a mind at work, acting and conscious of its activity, to be more certain than any material thing. And this was what it was all about: *the fact was* that his students *had learned* to speak and to write in French without the aid of explication. He had communicated nothing to them about his science, no explications of the roots and flexions of the French language. He hadn't even proceeded in the fashion of those reformer pedagogues who, like the preceptor in Rousseau's *Emile*, mislead their students the better to guide them, and who cunningly erect an obstacle course for the students to learn to negotiate themselves. He had left them alone with the text by Fénelon, a translation—not even interlinear like a schoolbook—and their will to learn French. He had only given them the order to pass through a forest whose openings and clearings he himself had not discovered. Necessity had constrained him to leave his intelligence entirely out of the picture—that mediating intelligence of the master that relays the printed intelligence of written words to the apprentice's. And, in one fell swoop, he had suppressed the imaginary distance that is the principle of pedagogical stultification. Everything had perforce been played out between the intelligence of Fénelon who had wanted to make a particular use of the French language, the intelligence of the translator who had wanted to give a Flemish equivalent, and the intelligence of the apprentices who wanted to learn French. And it had appeared that no other intelligence was necessary. Without thinking about it, he had made them discover this thing that he discovered with them: that all sentences, and consequently all the intelligences that produce them, are of the same nature. Understanding is never more than translating, that is, giving the equivalent of a text, but in no way its reason. There is nothing behind the written page, no false bottom that necessitates the work of an *other* intelligence, that of the explicator; no language of the master, no language of the language whose words and sentences are able to speak the reason of the words and sentences of a text. The Flemish students had furnished the proof: to speak about *Télémaque* they had at their disposition only the words of *Télémaque*. Fénelon's sentences alone are necessary to understand Fénelon's sentences and to express what one has understood about them. Learning and understanding are two ways of expressing the same act of translation. There is nothing beyond texts except the will to express, that is, to translate. If they had understood the language by learning Fénelon, it wasn't simply through the gymnastics of comparing the page on the left with the page on the right. It isn't the aptitude for changing columns that counts, but rather the capacity to say what one thinks in the words of others. If they had learned this from Fénelon, that was because the act of Fénelon the writer was itself one of translation: in order to translate a political lesson into a legendary narrative, Fénelon transformed into the French of his century Homer's Greek, Vergil's Latin, and the language, wise or naïve, of a hundred other texts, from children's stories to erudite history. He had applied to this double translation the same intelligence they employed in their turn to recount with the sentences of his book what they thought about his book.

But the intelligence that had allowed them to learn the French in *Télémaque* was the same they had used to learn their mother tongue: by observing and retaining, repeating and verifying, by relating what they were trying to know to what they already knew, by doing and reflecting about what they had done. They moved along in a manner one shouldn't move along—the way children move, blindly, figuring out riddles. And the question then became: wasn't it necessary to overturn the admissible order of intellectual values? Wasn't that shameful method of the riddle the true movement of human intelligence taking possession of its own power? Didn't its proscription indicate above all the will to divide the world of intelligence into two? The advocates of method oppose the nonmethod of chance to that of proceeding by reason. But what they want to prove is given in advance. They suppose a little animal who, bumping into things, explores a world that he isn't yet able to see and will only discern when they teach him to do so. But the human child is first of all a speaking being. The child who repeats the words he hears and the Flemish student "lost" in his *Télémaque* are not proceeding hit or miss. All their effort, all their exploration, is strained toward this: someone has addressed words to them that they want to recognize and respond to, not as students or as learned men, but as people; in the way you respond to someone speaking to you and not to someone examining you: under the sign of equality.

The fact was there: they had learned by themselves, without a master explicator. What has happened once is thenceforth always possible. This discovery could, after all, overturn the principles of the *professor* Jacotot. But Jacotot the man was in a better position to recognize what great variety can be expected from a human being. His father had been a butcher before keeping the accounts of his grandfather, the carpenter who had sent his grandson to college. He himself had been a professor of rhetoric when he had answered the call to arms in 1792. His companions' vote had made him an artillery captain, and he had showed himself to be a remarkable artilleryman. In 1793, at the Bureau of Powders, this Latinist became a chemistry instructor working toward the accelerated forming of workers being sent everywhere in the territory to apply Fourcroy's discoveries. At Fourcroy's own establishment, he had become acquainted with Vauquelin, the peasant's son who had trained himself to be a chemist without the knowledge of his boss. He had seen young people arrive at the Ecole Polytechnique who had been selected by improvised commissions on the dual basis of their liveliness of mind and their patriotism. And he had seen them become very good mathematicians, less through the calculations Monge and Lagrange explained to them than through those that they performed in front of them.* He himself had apparently profited from his administrative functions by gaining competence as a mathematician—a competence he had exercised later at the University of Dijon. Similarly, he had added Hebrew to the ancient languages he taught, and composed an *Essay on Hebrew Grammar*. He believed, God knows why, that that language had a future. And finally, he had gained for himself, reluctantly but with the greatest firmness, a competence at being a representative of the people. In short, he knew what the will of individuals and the peril of the country could engender in the way of unknown capacities, in circumstances where urgency demanded destroying the stages of explicative progression. He thought that this exceptional state, dictated by the nation's need, was no different in principle from the urgency that dictates the exploration of the world by the child or from that other urgency that constrains the singular path of learned men and inventors. Through the experiment of the child, the learned man, and the revolutionary, the method of *chance* so successfully practiced by the Flemish students revealed its second secret. The method of equality was above all a method of the will. One could learn by oneself and without a master explicator when one wanted to, propelled by one's own desire or by the constraint of the situation.

The Emancipatory Master

In this case, that constraint had taken the form of the command Jacotot had given. And it resulted in an important consequence, no longer for the students but for the master. The students had learned without a master explicator, but not, for all that, without a master. They didn't know how before, and

---

*Antoine François Fourcroy (1755–1809), chemist and politician, participated in the establishment of a rational nomenclature in chemistry. The principal work of the mathematician Joseph Louis de Lagrange (1736–1813) was the *Mécanique analytique* (1788). The mathematician Gaspard Monge (1746–1818) helped create the Ecole Normale and founded the Ecole Polytechnique.—TRANS.

now they knew how. Therefore, Jacotot had taught them something. And yet he had communicated nothing to them of his science. So it wasn't the master's science that the student learned. His mastery lay in the command that had enclosed the students in a closed circle from which they alone could break out. By leaving his intelligence out of the picture, he had allowed their intelligence to grapple with that of the book. Thus, the two functions that link the practice of the master explicator, that of the savant and that of the master had been dissociated. The two faculties in play during the act of learning, namely intelligence and will, had therefore also been separated, liberated from each other. A pure relationship of will to will had been established between master and student: a relationship wherein the master's domination resulted in an entirely liberated relationship between the intelligence of the student and that of the book—the intelligence of the book that was also the thing in common, the egalitarian intellectual link between master and student. This device allowed the jumbled categories of the pedagogical act to be sorted out, and explicative stultification to be precisely defined. There is stultification whenever one intelligence is subordinated to another. A person—and a child in particular—may need a master when his own will is not strong enough to set him on track and keep him there. But that subjection is purely one of will over will. It becomes stultification when it links an intelligence to another intelligence. In the act of teaching and learning there are two wills and two intelligences. We will call their coincidence *stultification*. In the experimental situation Jacotot created, the student was linked to a will, Jacotot's, and to an intelligence, the book's—the two entirely distinct. We will call the known and maintained difference of the two relations—the act of an intelligence obeying only itself even while the will obeys another will—*emancipation*.

This pedagogical experiment created a rupture with the logic of all pedagogies. The pedagogues' practice is based on the opposition between science and ignorance. The methods chosen to render the ignorant person learned may differ: strict or gentle methods, traditional or modern, active or passive; the efficiency of these methods can be compared. From this point of view, we could, at first glance, compare the speed of Jacotot's students with the slowness of traditional methods. But in reality there was nothing to compare. The confrontation of methods presupposes a minimal agreement on the goals of the pedagogical act: the transmission of the master's knowledge to the students. But Jacotot had transmitted nothing. He had not used any method. The method was purely the student's. And whether one learns French more quickly or less quickly is in itself a matter of little consequence. The comparison was no longer between methods but rather between two uses of intelligence and two conceptions of the intellectual order. The rapid route was not that of a better pedagogy. It was another route, that of liberty—that route that Jacotot had experimented with in the armies of Year II, the fabrication of powders or the founding of the Ecole Polytechnique, the route of liberty responding to the urgency of the peril, but just as much to a confidence in the intellectual capacity of any human being. Beneath the pedagogical relation of ignorance to science, the more fundamental philosophical relation of stultification to emancipation must be recognized. There were thus not two but four terms in play. The act of learning could be produced according to four variously combined determinations: by an emancipatory master or by a stultifying one, by a learned master or by an ignorant one.

The last proposition was the most difficult to accept. It goes without saying that a scientist might do science without explicating it. But how can we admit that an ignorant person might induce science in another? Even Jacotot's experiment was ambiguous because of his position as a professor of French. But since it had at least shown that it wasn't the master's knowledge that instructed the student, then nothing prevented the master from teaching something other than his science, something he didn't know. Joseph Jacotot applied himself to varying the experiment, to repeating on purpose what chance had once produced. He began to teach two subjects at which he was notably incompetent: painting and the piano. Law students would have liked him to be given a vacant chair in their faculty. But the University of Louvain was already worried about this extravagant lecturer, for whom students were deserting the magisterial courses, in favor of coming, evenings, to crowd into a much too small room, lit by only two candles, in order to hear: "I must teach you that I have nothing to teach you."[2] The authority they consulted thus responded that he saw no point in calling this teaching. Jacotot was experimenting, precisely, with the gap between accreditation and act. Rather than teaching a law course in French, he taught the students to litigate in Flemish. They litigated very well, but he still didn't know Flemish.

The Circle of Power

The experiment seemed to him sufficient to shed light: one can teach what one doesn't know if the student is emancipated, that is to say, if he is obliged to use his own intelligence. The master is he who encloses an intelligence in the arbitrary circle from which it can only break out by becoming necessary to itself. To emancipate an ignorant person, one must be, and one need only be, emancipated oneself, that is to say, conscious of the true power of the human mind. The ignorant person will learn by himself what the master doesn't know if the master believes he can and obliges him to realize his capacity: a circle of *power* homologous to the circle of powerlessness that ties the student to the explicator of the old method (to be called from now on, simply, the Old Master). But the relation of forces is very particular. The circle of powerlessness is always already there: it is the very workings of the social world, hidden in the evident difference between ignorance and science. The circle of power, on the other hand, can only take effect by being made public. But it can only appear as a tautology or an absurdity. How can the learned master ever understand that he can teach what he doesn't know as successfully as what he does know? He cannot but take that increase in intellectual power as a devaluation of his science. And the ignorant one, on his side, doesn't believe himself capable of learning by himself, still less of being able to teach another ignorant person. Those excluded from the world of intelligence themselves subscribe to the verdict of their exclusion. In short, the circle of emancipation must be *begun*.

Here lies the paradox. For if you think about it a little, the "method" he was proposing is the oldest in the world, and it never stops being verified every day, in all the circumstances where an individual must learn something without any means of having it explained to him. There is no one on earth who hasn't learned something by himself and without a master explicator. Let's call this way of learning "universal teaching" and say of it: "In reality, universal teaching has existed since the beginning of the world, alongside all the explicative methods. This teaching, by oneself, has, in reality, been what has formed all great men." But this is the strange part: "Everyone has done this experiment a thousand times in his life, and yet it has never occurred to someone to say to someone else: I've learned many things without explanations, I think that you can too. . . . Neither I nor anyone in the world has ventured to draw on this fact to teach others."[3] To the intelligence sleeping in each of us, it would suffice to say: *age quod agis*, continue to do what you are doing, "learn the fact, imitate it, know yourself, this is how nature works."[4] Methodically repeat the method of chance that gave you the measure of your power. The same intelligence is at work in all the acts of the human mind.

But this is the most difficult leap. This method is practiced of necessity by everyone, but no one wants to recognize it, no one wants to cope with the intellectual revolution it signifies. The social circle, the order of things, prevents it from being recognized for what it is: the true method by which everyone learns and by which everyone can take the measure of his capacity. One must dare to recognize it and pursue the *open* verification of its power—otherwise, the method of powerlessness, the Old Master, will last as long as the order of things.

Who would want to begin? In Jacotot's day there were all kinds of men of goodwill who were preoccupied with instructing the people: rulers wanted to elevate the people above their brutal appetites, revolutionaries wanted to lead them to the consciousness of their rights; progressives wished to narrow, through instruction, the gap between the classes; industrialists dreamed of giving, through instruction, the most intelligent among the people the means of social promotion. All these good intentions came up against an obstacle: the common man had very little time and even less money to devote to acquiring this instruction. Thus, what was sought was the economic means of diffusing the minimum of instruction judged necessary for the individual and sufficient for the amelioration of the laboring population as a whole. Among progressives and industrialists the favored method was mutual teaching. This allowed a great number of students, assembled from a vast locale, to be divided up into smaller groups headed by the more advanced among them, who were promoted to the rank of monitors. In this way, the master's orders and lessons radiated out, relayed by the monitors, into the whole population to be instructed. Friends of progress liked what they saw: this was how science extended from the summits to the most modest levels of intelligence. Happiness and liberty would trickle down in its wake.

That sort of progress, for Jacotot, smelled of the bridle. "A perfected riding-school," he said. He had a different notion of mutual teaching in mind: that each ignorant person could become for another ignorant person the master who would reveal to him his intellectual power. More precisely, his problem wasn't the instruction of the people: one *instructed* the recruits enrolled under one's banner, subalterns who must be able to understand orders, the people one wanted to govern—in the progressive way, of course, without divine right and only according to the hierarchy of *capacities*. His own problem was that of *emancipation*: that every common person might conceive his human dignity, take the measure of his intellectual capacity, and decide how to use it. The friends of Instruction were certain that true liberty was conditioned on it. After all, they recognized that they should give instruction to the people, even at the risk of disputing among themselves which instruction they would give. Jacotot did not see what kind of liberty for the people could result from the dutifulness of their instructors. On the contrary, he sensed in all this a new form of stultification. Whoever teaches without emancipating stultifies. And whoever emancipates doesn't have to worry about what the emancipated person learns. He will learn what he wants, nothing maybe. He will know he can learn because the same intelligence is at work in all the productions of the human mind, and a man can always understand another man's words. Jacotot's printer had a retarded son. They had despaired of making something of him. Jacotot taught him Hebrew. Later the child became an excellent lithographer. It goes without saying that he never used the Hebrew for anything—except to know what more gifted and learned minds never knew: *it wasn't Hebrew.*

The matter was thus clear. This was not a method for instructing the people; it was a benefit to be announced to the poor: they could do everything any man could. It sufficed only to *announce* it. Jacotot decided to devote himself to this. He proclaimed that one could teach what one didn't know, and that a poor and ignorant father could, if he was emancipated, conduct the education of his children, without the aid of any master explicator. And he indicated the way of that "universal teaching"—*to learn something and to relate to it all the rest by this principle: all men have equal intelligence.*

People were affected in Louvain, in Brussels, and in La Haye; they took the mail carriage from Paris and Lyon; they came from England and Prussia to hear the news; it was proclaimed in Saint Petersburg and New Orleans. The word reached as far as Rio de Janeiro. For several years polemic raged, and the Republic of knowledge was shaken at its very foundations.

All this because a learned man, a renowned man of science and a virtuous family man, had gone crazy for not knowing Flemish.

2 | The Ignorant One's Lesson

Let's go ashore, then, with Telemachus onto Calyp-
so's island. Let's make our way with one of the visitors into the
madman's lair: into Miss Marcellis's institution in Louvain; into
the home of Mr. Deschuyfeleere, a tanner transformed by Jacotot into a Latinist; into the Ecole Normale Militaire in Louvain, where the philosopher-prince Frederick of Orange had put
the Founder of universal teaching in charge of educating future
military instructors:

"Imagine recruits sitting on benches, murmuring in unison: 'Calypso,' 'Calypso could,' 'Calypso could not,' etc., etc.; two months
later they knew how to read, write, and count. . . . During this primary education, the one was taught English, the other German, this
one fortification, that one chemistry, etc., etc."
"Did the Founder know all these things?"
"Not at all, but we explained them to him, and I can assure you
he profited greatly from the Ecole Normale."
"But I'm confused. Did you all, then, know chemistry?"
"No, but we learned it, and we gave him lessons in it. That's universal teaching. It's the disciple that makes the master."[1]

There is an order in madness, as in everything. Let's begin,
then, at the beginning: *Télémaque*. "Everything is in everything," says the madman. And his critics add: "And everything
is in *Télémaque*." Because *Télémaque* was apparently the book

that could do anything. Does the student want to learn how to read? Does he want to learn English or German, the art of litigation or of combat? The madman, imperturbably, will put a copy of *Télémaque* in his hands and the student will begin to repeat, "Calypso," "Calypso could," "Calypso could not," and so on, until he knows the prescribed number of volumes of *Télémaque* and can recount them. He must be able to talk about everything he learns—the form of the letters, the placement or endings of words, the images, the reasoning, the characters' feelings, the moral lessons—to say *what he sees, what he thinks about it, what he makes of it.* There was only one rule: he must be able to show, in the book, the materiality of everything he says. He will be asked to write compositions and perform improvisations under the same conditions: he must use the words and turns of phrase in the book to construct his sentences; he must show, in the book, the facts on which his reasoning is based. In short, the master must be able to verify in the book the materiality of everything the student says.

The Island of the Book

The book. *Télémaque* or another one. Chance placed *Télémaque* at Jacotot's disposal; convenience told him to keep it. *Télémaque* has been translated into many languages and is easily available in bookstores. It isn't the greatest masterpiece of the French language; but the style is pure, the vocabulary varied, and the moral severe. In it one learns mythology and geography. And behind the French "translation," one can hear the echo of Vergil's Latin and Homer's Greek. In short, it's a classic, one of those books in which a language presents the essential of its forms and its powers. A book that is a *totality*: a center to which one can attach everything new one learns; a circle in which one can *understand* each of these new things, find the ways to say what one sees in it, what one thinks about it, what one makes of it. This is the first principle of universal teaching: one must learn something and relate everything else to it. And first *some-*

thing must be learned. Would La Palice say as much?* La Palice maybe, but the Old Master would say: such and such a thing must be learned, and then this other thing and after that, this other. Selection, progression, incompletion: these are his principles. We learn rules and elements, then apply them to some chosen reading passages, and then do some exercises based on the acquired rudiments. Then we graduate to a higher level: other rudiments, another book, other exercises, another professor. At each stage the abyss of ignorance is dug again; the professor fills it in before digging another. Fragments add up, detached pieces of an explicator's knowledge that put the student on a trail, following a master with whom he will never catch up. The book is never whole, the lesson is never finished. The master always keeps a piece of learning—that is to say, a piece of the student's ignorance—up his sleeve. I understood that, says the satisfied student. You think so, corrects the master. In fact, there's a difficulty here that I've been sparing you until now. We will explain it when we get to the corresponding lesson. What does this mean? asks the curious student. I could tell you, responds the master, but it would be premature: you wouldn't understand at all. It will be explained to you next year. The master is always a length ahead of the student, who always feels that in order to go farther he must have another master, supplementary explications. Thus does the triumphant Achilles drag Hector's corpse, attached to his chariot, around the city of Troy. Reasoned progression of knowledge is an indefinitely reproduced mutilation. "Any man who is taught is only half a man."[2]

Don't ask if the little educated child suffers from this mutilation. The system's genius is to transform loss into profit. The child *advances*. He has been taught, therefore he has learned, therefore he can forget. Behind him the abyss of ignorance is being dug again. But here's the amazing part: from now on the

---

*Jacques de Chabannes La Palice (1470–1525) was celebrated in his own time as a military leader, but what made him immortal was a naïve song composed by his soldiers, which ended with the line: "Fifteen minutes before his death/He was still alive." In French, "the words of La Palice" refers to any self-evident formulation.—TRANS.

ignorance is someone else's. What he has forgotten, he has surpassed. He no longer has to spell out loud or stumble his way
through a lesson like those vulgar intelligences and the children
in beginning classes. People aren't parrots in his school. We
don't load the memory, we form the intelligence. I understood,
says the child, I am not a parrot. The more he forgets, the more
evident it is to him that he understands. The more intelligent
he becomes, the more he can peer down from on high at those
he has surpassed, those who remain in the antechamber of learning, in front of the mute book, those who repeat, because they
are not intelligent enough to *understand*. This is the genius of
the explicators: they attach the creature they have rendered inferior with the strongest chains in the land of stultification—
the child's consciousness of his own superiority.

This consciousness, moreover, doesn't kill off good feelings.
The little educated child will perhaps be moved by the ignorance of the common people and will want to work at instructing them. He will know it is difficult to deal with minds hardened by routine or befuddled by unmethodicalness. But if he is
devoted, he will know that there is a kind of explication adapted
to each category in the hierarchy of intelligence: he will come
down *to their level*.

But now here is another story. The madman—the Founder,
as his followers called him—comes on stage with his *Télémaque*,
a book, a thing.

Take it and read it, he says to the poor person.

I don't know how to read, answers the poor person. How
would I understand what is written in the book?

As you have understood all things up until now: by comparing two facts. Here is a fact that I will tell you, the first sentence
of the book: "Calypso could not be consoled after the departure
of Ulysses." Repeat: "Calypso," "Calypso could" . . . Now,
here is a second fact: the words are written there. Don't you
recognize anything? The first word I said to you was Calypso;
wouldn't that also be the first word on the page? Look at it
closely, until you are sure of always recognizing it in the middle

of a crowd of other words. In order to do this you must *tell* me
everything you see there. There are signs that a hand traced on
paper, signs whose type was assembled by a hand at the printer's. Tell me "the story of the adventures, that is, the comings
and goings, the detours—in a word, the trajectory of the pen
that wrote this word on paper or of the engraving tool that en-
graved it onto the copper."[3] Would you know how to recognize
the letter O that one of my students—a locksmith by profession—calls "the round," the letter L that he calls "the square"?
Tell me the form of each letter as you would describe the form
of an object or of an unknown place. Don't say that you can't.
You know how to see, how to speak, you know how to show,
you can remember. What more is needed? An absolute attention
for seeing and seeing again, saying and repeating. Don't try to
fool me or fool yourself. Is that really what you saw? *What do
you think about it?* Aren't you a thinking being? Or do you think
you are all body? "The founder Sganarelle changed all that. . . .
You have a soul like me."[4] There will be time afterward to talk
about what the book talks about: what do you think of Calypso,
of sadness, of a goddess, of an eternal spring? Show me what
makes you say what you say.

The book prevents escape. The route the student will take is
unknown. But we know what he cannot escape: the exercise of
his liberty. We know too that the master won't have the right
to stand anywhere else—only at the door. The student must see
everything for himself, compare and compare, and always respond to a three-part question: what do you see? what do you
think about it? what do you make of it? And so on, to infinity.

But that infinity is no longer the master's secret; it is the student's journey. The book is finished. It is a totality that the student holds in his hand, that he can span entirely with a glance.
There is nothing the master can hide from him, and nothing he
can hide from the master's gaze. The circle forbids cheating, and
above all, that great cheat: incapacity. *I can't, I don't understand.*
There is nothing to understand. Everything is in the book. One
has only to recount it—the form of each sign, the adventures

of each sentence, the lesson of each volume. One must begin to
speak. Don't say that you can't. You know how to say "I can't."
Say in its place "Calypso could not," and you're off. You're off
on a route that you already knew, and that you should follow
always without giving up. Don't say: "I can't." Or then, learn
to say it in the manner of Calypso, in the manner of Telemachus, of Narbal, of Idomeneus. The other circle has begun, the
circle of power. You will never run out of ways to say "I can't,"
and soon you will able to say everything.

A voyage in a circle. It's understood that the adventures of
Ulysses's son form the manual, and Calypso the first word. Calypso, *the hidden one.* But precisely what must be discovered is
that there is nothing hidden, no words underneath words, no
language that tells the truth of language. Signs and still more
signs are learned, sentences and still more sentences. Ready-
made sentences are repeated. Entire books are learned by heart.
And the Old Master becomes indignant: so this is what learning
something means for you. First, your children repeat like parrots. They cultivate only one faculty, memory, while we exercise
intelligence, taste, and imagination. Your children learn *by
heart.* That's your first mistake. And this is your second: your
children *don't learn* by heart. You say that they do, but that's
impossible. Human brains in general, and those of children in
particular, are incapable of such an effort of memory.

A circular argument. The discourse of one circle to another.
The propositions must be overturned. The Old Master says that
a child's memory is incapable of such efforts because powerlessness, in general, is its slogan. It says that memory is something
other than intelligence or imagination and, in so doing, it uses
an ordinary weapon against those that want to prevail over powerlessness: division. It believes memory to be weak because it
doesn't believe in the power of human intelligence. It believes
it inferior because it believes in inferiors and superiors. In the
end its double argument amounts to this: there are inferiors and
superiors; inferiors can't do what superiors can.

The Old Master knows only this. It depends on inequality,

but not the inequality that acknowledges the Prince's decree, the inequality that goes without saying, that is in all heads and in all sentences. For that, it has its gentle weapon, difference: *this is not that, this is far from that, one cannot compare* . . . Memory is not intelligence; to repeat is not to know; comparison isn't reason; there is the ground and the background. Any flour can be ground up in the mill of distinction. And the argument can thus be modernized and extended to the scientific as well as to the humanitarian: there are stages in the development of intelligence; a child's intelligence is not an adult's; a child's intelligence should not be overburdened—one runs the risk of injuring his health, his faculties. The Old Master demands only that he be granted his negations and his differences: this is not that, this is something different, this is more, this is less. And this is enough to exalt all the thrones of the hierarchy of intelligence.

Calypso and the Locksmith

Let the Old Master have his say. Let's look at the facts. There is a will that commands and an intelligence that obeys. Let's call the act that makes an intelligence proceed under the absolute constraint of a will *attention*. It makes no difference whether the act is directed at the form of a letter to be recognized, a sentence to be memorized, a relation to be found between two mathematical entities, or the elements of a speech to be composed. There is not one faculty that records, another that understands, another that judges. The locksmith who calls the letter O "the round," and L "the square" is already thinking about relations. And inventing is not of another order than remembering. Let the explicators "form" the children's "taste" and "imagination"; let them expound on the "genius" of creators. We will be content to do as creators do: like Racine, who memorized, translated, repeated, and imitated Euripides; Bossuet, who did the same with Tertullian; Rousseau with Amyot; Boileau with Horace and Juvenal; like Demosthenes, who copied

Thucydides eight times; Hooft, who read Tacitus fifty-two
times; Seneca, who recommended that the same book be read
and reread; Haydn, who recreated six of Bach's sonatas over and
over; Michelangelo, who spent his time redoing the same torso
again and again.[5] Power cannot be divided up. There is only one
power, that of saying and speaking, of paying attention to what
one sees and says. One learns sentences and more sentences; one
discovers facts, that is, relations between things, and still other
relations that are all of the same nature; one learns to combine
letters, words, sentences, ideas. It will not be said that one has
acquired science, that one knows truth or has become a genius.
But it will be known that, in the intellectual order, one can do
what any man can do.

This is what *everything is in everything* means: the tautology of
power. All the power of language is in the totality of a book.
All knowledge of oneself as an intelligence is in the mastery of
a book, a chapter, a sentence, a word. Everything is in everything and everything is in *Télémaque*, scoff the critics, and, to
catch the disciples off guard, they ask, Is everything also in the
first volume of *Télémaque*? And in its first word? Is mathematics
in *Télémaque*? And in the first word of *Télémaque*? And the disciple feels the ground slip out from under him and calls on the
master for help: what should he answer?

You should have answered that you believe all human works to be in
the word Calypso since this word is a work of human intelligence.
He who calculated fractions is the same intellectual being as he who
made the word Calypso. The artist knew Greek; he chose a word that
meant "crafty," "hidden." The artist resembles the one who imagined
the ways of writing the word we're talking about. He resembles the
one who made the paper on which we write, the one who uses pens
to the same purpose, the one who sharpens the pens with a penknife,
the one who made the penknife out of iron, the one who procured the
iron, the one who made the ink, the one who printed the word Calypso, the one who made the printing machine, the one who gener-
alized the explications, the one who made the printing ink, etc., etc.,
etc. All sciences, all art, anatomy, dynamics, and so on, are the fruits
of the same intelligence who made the word Calypso. A philosopher

arriving in an unknown land would know it was inhabited when he saw a geometrical figure in the sand. "These are human footprints," he says. His companions believe him mad because the lines he shows them don't look like a footprint. The scholars of the perfected nineteenth century open their startled eyes wide when someone points a finger at the word Calypso and tells them, "A human hand is there." I bet that the man sent from the Ecole Normale in France, looking at the word Calypso, would say: "That doesn't have the shape of a hand." *"Everything is in everything."*[6]

Here is everything that is *in* Calypso: the power of intelligence that is in any human manifestation. The same intelligence makes nouns and mathematical signs. What's more, it also makes signs and reasonings. There aren't two sorts of minds. There is inequality in the *manifestations* of intelligence, according to the greater or lesser energy communicated to the intelligence by the will for discovering and combining new relations; but there is no hierarchy of *intellectual capacity*. Emancipation is becoming conscious of this equality of *nature*. This is what opens the way to all adventure in the land of knowledge. It is a matter of daring to be adventurous, and not whether one learns more or less well or more or less quickly. The "Jacotot method" is not better; it is different. That's why the procedures used matter very little in themselves. It could be *Télémaque*, or it could be something else. One begins with the text and not with grammar, with entire words and not with syllables. It is not that it is absolutely necessary to learn this way to learn better, and that the Jacotot method is the forefather of the global method. In fact, it's much faster to start with "Calypso" and not with the A,B,Cs. But the speed won is only an effect of power gained, a consequence of the emancipatory principle. "The Old Master begins with letters because he directs students according to the principle of intellectual inequality, and especially the intellectual inferiority of children. He believes that letters are easier to distinguish than words; this is wrong, but this is what he thinks. He believes that a child's intelligence is only able to learn C, A, C, and that an adult, that is to say a superior, intelligence is necessary to learn Calypso."[7] In short,

B, A, B, like Calypso, is a flag; *inability* versus *ability*. Spelling is an act of contrition before being a way of learning. That's why one could change the order of the procedures without changing anything in the principles.

The Old Master might one day take it into his head to train to read by words and only then, maybe, would we have our students learn how to spell them. And what would result from this apparent change of posture? Nothing. Our students would be no less emancipated and the children of the Old Master no less stultified. . . . The Old Master doesn't stultify his students by making them spell; he stultifies by telling them that they can't spell by themselves. Making them read by words won't emancipate them; it will deaden them because he will be very careful to tell them that their young intelligence can't do without the explications he pulls out of his aged brain. It is thus not the procedure, the course, the manner, that emancipates or stultifies; it's the principle. The principle of inequality, the old principle, stultifies no matter what one does; the principle of equality, the Jacotot principle, emancipates no matter what procedure, book, or fact it is applied to.[8]

The problem is to reveal an intelligence to itself. *Anything* can be used. *Télémaque.* Or a prayer or a song that the child or the ignorant one knows by heart. There is always something the ignorant one knows that can be used as a point of comparison, something to which a new thing to be learned can be related. The locksmith who opens his eyes wide when told he can read bears witness to this. He doesn't even know the alphabet. Let him take the time to glance at the calendar. Doesn't he know the order of the months and can't he thus figure out January, February, March. He knows how to count a little. And what's to prevent him from counting softly while following the lines in order to recognize in written form what he already knows? He knows he is called William and that his birthday is January 16th. He will soon know how to find the word. He knows that February has only twenty-eight days. He sees that one column is shorter than the others and he will recognize "28." And so on. There is always something that the master can ask him to find, something about which he can question him and thus verify the work of his intelligence.

The Master and Socrates

These are in fact the master's two fundamental acts. He *interrogates*, he demands speech, that is to say, the manifestation of an intelligence that wasn't aware of itself or that had given up. And he *verifies* that the work of the intelligence is done with attention, that the words don't say just anything in order to escape from the constraint. Is a highly skilled, very learned master necessary to perform this? On the contrary, the learned master's science makes it very difficult for him not to *spoil* the method. He knows the response, and his questions lead the student to it naturally. This is the secret of good masters: through their questions, they discreetly guide the student's intelligence—discreetly enough to make it work, but not to the point of leaving it to itself. There is a Socrates sleeping in every explicator. And it must be very clear how the Jacotot method— that is to say, the student's method—differs radically from the method of the Socratic master. Through his interrogations, Socrates leads Meno's slave to recognize the mathematical truths that lie within himself. This may be the path to learning, but it is in no way a path to emancipation. On the contrary, Socrates must take the slave by his hand so that the latter can find what is inside himself. The demonstration of his knowledge is just as much the demonstration of his powerlessness: he will never walk by himself, unless it is to illustrate the master's lesson. In this case, Socrates interrogates a slave who is destined to remain one.

The Socratic method is thus a perfected form of stultification. Like all learned masters, Socrates interrogates in order to instruct. But whoever wishes to emancipate someone must interrogate him in the manner of men and not in the manner of scholars, in order to be instructed, not to instruct. And that can only be performed by someone who effectively knows no more than the student, who has never made the voyage before him: the ignorant master. There's no risk of this master sparing the child the time necessary to account for the word Calypso. But what does he have to do with Calypso and how would he even understand anything about it? Let's forget Calypso for a moment. Who is the child who hasn't heard the Lord's Prayer, who hasn't learned the words by heart? In this way the thing is found, and the poor and ignorant father who wants to teach his son to read will not be embarrassed. He will certainly find some obliging person in the neighborhood, someone literate enough to copy the prayer for him. With this, the father or the mother can begin the child's instruction by asking him where the word Our is. "If the child is attentive, he will say that the first word on the paper must be Our, since it is the first word in the sentence. Father will necessarily be the second word; the child will be able to compare, distinguish, know these two words and recognize them everywhere."[9] Who is the father or mother who would not know how to ask the child, struggling with the text of the prayer, what he sees, what he makes of it or what he can say about it, and what he thinks about what he's saying or doing? It's the same way he would ask a neighbor about the tool he holds in his hand and how it is used. To teach what one doesn't know is simply to ask questions about what one doesn't know. Science isn't needed to ask such questions. The ignorant one can ask anything, and for the voyager in the land of signs, his questions alone will be true questions compelling the autonomous exercise of his intelligence.

Granted, replies the critic. But that which makes the interrogator forceful also makes him incompetent as a verifier. How will he know if the child is losing his way? The father or mother can always ask the child: show me "Father" or "Heaven." But how can they verify if the child has pointed to the right word? The difficulty can only get worse as the child advances—if he advances—in his training. Won't the ignorant master and the ignorant student be playing out the fable of the blind man leading the blind?

The Power of the Ignorant

Let's begin by reassuring the critics: we will not make of the ignorant one the fount of an innate science, and especially not of a science of the people as opposed to that of the scholar. One must be learned to judge the results of the work, to verify the student's science. The ignorant one himself will do *less* and *more* at the same time. He will not verify what the student has found; he will verify that the student has searched. He will judge whether or not he has paid attention. For one need only be human to judge the fact of work. Just like the philosopher who "recognizes" human footprints in the lines in the sand, the mother knows how to see "in his eyes, in the child's features, when he is doing work, when he is pointing to the words in a sentence, if he is attentive to what he is doing."[10] The ignorant master must demand from his student that he prove to him that he has studied attentively. Is this insignificant? Think about everything the demand implies for the student in the way of an endless task. Think about the intelligence it can also grant to the ignorant examiner: "What prevents the *ignorant* but *emancipated* mother from noticing all the times that she asks the child where 'Father' is, whether or not he always points to the same word; what prevents her hiding the word and asking, what is the word under my finger? Etc., etc."[11]

A pious image, a housewife's recipe . . . This is how the official spokesman of the explicative tribe judged it: "*One can teach what one doesn't know* is still a housewife's motto."[12] We will argue that "maternal intuition" does not exert any domestic privilege here. The finger that hides the word Father is the same that is *in* Calypso, the hidden or the crafty: the mark of human intelligence, the most elementary ruse of its reason—the true reason, the one proper to each and common to all, this reason that is manifested in an exemplary fashion whenever the ignorant one's knowledge and the master's ignorance, by becoming equal, demonstrate the powers of intellectual equality. "Man is an animal who can tell very well when a speaker doesn't know what he's talking about"; "that ability is what unites us as humans."[13] The practice of the ignorant master is not the simple expedient of allowing the poor who have neither time, nor money, nor knowledge, to educate their children. It is the crucial experiment that liberates the pure powers of reason wherever science does not lend a hand. What one ignorant person can perform once, all ignorant people can always perform—because there is no hierarchy in ignorance. What ignorant people and learned people can both do can be called the power of the intelligent being as such.

This power of equality is at once one of duality and one of community. There is no intelligence where there is aggregation, the *binding* of one mind to another. There is intelligence where each person acts, tells what he is doing, and gives the means of verifying the reality of his action. The thing in common, placed between two minds, is the gauge of that equality, and this in two ways. A material thing is first of all "the only bridge of communication between two minds."[14] The bridge is a passage, but it is also distance maintained. The materiality of the book keeps two minds at an equal distance, whereas explication is the annihilation of one mind by another. But the thing is also an always available source of material verification: the ignorant examiner's art is to "bring the examinee back to the material objects, to a *thing* that he can verify with his senses."[15] The examinee is always beholden to a verification in the open book, in the materiality of each word, the curve of each sign. The thing, the book, prevents cheating by both the ignorant and the learned. This is why the ignorant master can from time to time extend his competence to the point of verifying, not the child's knowledge, but the attention he gives to what he is doing and saying.

In this way you can even be of service to one of your neighbors who finds himself, because of circumstances beyond his control, forced to send his son to school. If the neighbor asks you to verify the young student's knowledge, you need not hesitate to perform this inquiry, even though you have had no schooling. "What are you learning, my little friend?" you will ask the child. "Greek." "What?" "Aesop." "What?" "The Fables." "Which ones do you know?" "The first one." "Where is the first word?" "There it is." "Give me your book. Tell me the fourth word. Write it. What you have written doesn't look like the fourth word in the book. Neighbor, the child doesn't know what he says he knows. This is proof that he wasn't paying attention while studying or while displaying what he says he knows. Advise him to study; I will return and tell you if he is learning the Greek that I myself don't know, that I don't even know how to read."[16]

This is the way that the ignorant master can instruct the learned one as well as the ignorant one: by verifying that he is always searching. Whoever looks always finds. He doesn't necessarily find what he was looking for, and even less what he was supposed to find. But he finds something new to relate to the *thing* that he already knows. What is essential is the continuous vigilance, the attention that never subsides without irrationality setting in—something that the learned one, like the ignorant one, excels at. The master is he who keeps the researcher on his own route, the one that he alone is following and keeps following.

To Each His Own

Still, to verify this kind of research, one must know what seeking or researching means. And this is the heart of the method. To emancipate someone else, one must be emancipated oneself. One must know oneself to be a voyager of the mind, similar to all other voyagers: an intellectual subject participating in the power common to intellectual beings.

How does one accede to this self-knowledge? "A peasant, an artisan (father of a family), will be intellectually emancipated if he thinks about what he is and what he does in the social order."[17] This assertion will seem simple, and even simplistic, to whoever ignores the weight of philosophy's old commandment, from the mouth of Plato, on the artisan's destiny: Don't do anything other than *your own affair*, which is not in any way *thinking*, but simply *making* that thing that exhausts the definition of your being; if you are a shoemaker, make shoes—and make children who will do the same. The Delphic oracle was not speaking to you when it said, Know yourself. And even if the playful divinity had fun mixing a little gold into your child's soul, it is the golden race, the guardians of the city, who will take on the task of raising him to be one of theirs.

The age of progress undoubtedly wanted to shake the rigidity from the old commandment. Along with the Encyclopedists, this age understands that nothing is done by routine anymore, not even artisans' work. And it knows that there is no social actor, no matter how insignificant, who is not at the same time a thinking being. Citizen Destutt-Tracy recalled this at the dawning of the new century: "Every speaking man has ideas of ideology, grammar, logic, and eloquence. Every man who acts has principles of private morals and social morals. Every being who merely vegetates has his notions of physics and arithmetic; and simply because he lives with those like himself, he has his little collection of historical facts and his way of evaluating them."[18]

It is thus impossible for shoemakers just to make shoes, that they not also be, in their manner, grammarians, moralists, or physicists. And this is the first problem: as long as peasants and artisans form moral, mathematical, or physical notions based on their environmental routine or their chance encounters, the reasoned march of progress will be doubly at risk: slowed down by men of routine and superstition, or disrupted by the haste of violent men. Therefore, a minimum of instruction, drawn from the principles of reason, science, and the general interest, is necessary to put sane notions into heads that would otherwise form faulty ones. And it goes without saying that the enterprise will be all the more profitable if it removes the son of a peasant or artisan from the natural milieu that produces those false ideas. But this evidence immediately runs up against a contradiction: the child who must be removed from his routine and from superstition must nevertheless be returned to his activity and his condition. And since its dawning, the age of progress has been alert to the mortal danger of separating the child of the people from the condition to which he is destined and from the ideas that hold fast in that condition. Thus the age turns back and forth within this contradiction: that all the sciences are now known to be founded on simple principles available to all the minds who want to make use of them, provided they follow the right method. But the same nature that opens up a career in science to all minds wants a social order where the classes are separated and where individuals conform to the social state that is their destiny.

The solution to this contradiction is found in the ordered balance of instruction and moral education, the dividing up of the roles that fall to the schoolmaster and to the father of the family. Using the light of instruction, the first chases away the false ideas the child receives from his parental milieu; the second, by moral education, chases away the extravagant aspirations the schoolchild would like to extract from his young science and take back to his life condition. The father, incapable of drawing on his own experience to further his child's intellectual instruction, is, on the other hand, all-powerful in teaching him, by word and example, the virtue of remaining in his condition. The family is at once the nucleus of intellectual incapacity and the principle of ethical objectivity. This double character translates into a double limitation on the artisan's self-consciousness: the consciousness of what he *does* is drawn from a science that is not his own; the consciousness of what he *is* leads him back to doing nothing other than his own task.

Let us say it more simply: the harmonious balance of instruction and moral education is that of a double stultification. Emancipation is precisely the opposite of this; it is each man becoming conscious of his nature as an intellectual subject; it is the Cartesian formula of equality read backwards. "Descartes said, 'I think, therefore I am'; and this noble thought of the great philosopher is one of the principles of universal teaching.

We turn his thought around and say: 'I am a man, therefore I think.' "[19] The reversal equates "man" with *cogito*. Thought is not an attribute of the thinking substance; it is an attribute of *humanity*. To transform "Know yourself" into the principle of emancipation of any human being, it is necessary to activate, against the Platonic interdiction, one of the fantastic etymologies of the *Cratylus*: man, the *anthropos*, is the being who *examines what he sees*, who knows himself in so reflecting on his act.[20] The whole practice of universal teaching is summed up in the question: what do you think about it? Its whole power lies in the consciousness of emancipation that it realizes in the master and gives birth to in the student. The father could emancipate his son if he begins by knowing himself, that is to say, by examining the intellectual acts of which he is the subject, by noticing the manner in which he uses, in these acts, his power as a thinking being.

The consciousness of emancipation is above all the inventory of the ignorant one's intellectual capabilities. He knows his language. He also knows how to use it to protest against his state or to interrogate those who know, or who believe they know, more than he knows. He knows his trade, his tools, and their uses; he would be able to perfect them if need be. He must begin to reflect on his abilities and on the manner in which he acquired them.

Let's take the exact measure of that reflection. It is not about opposing manual knowledge, the knowledge of the people, the intelligence of the tool and of the worker, to the science of schools or the rhetoric of the elite. It is not about asking who built seven-gated Thebes as a way to vindicate the place of constructors and makers in the social order. On the contrary, it is about recognizing that there are not two levels of intelligence, that any human work of art is the practice of the same intellectual potential. In all cases, it is a question of observing, comparing, and combining, of making and noticing how one has done it. What is possible is reflection: that return to oneself that is not pure contemplation but rather an unconditional attention to one's intellectual acts, to the route they follow and to the possibility of always moving forward by bringing to bear the same intelligence on the conquest of new territories. He who makes a distinction between the manual work of the worker or the common man and clouds of rhetoric remains stultified. The fabrication of clouds is a human work of art that demands as much—neither more nor less—labor and intellectual attention as the fabrication of shoes or locks. The academician Lerminier expounded on the intellectual incapacity of the people. Lerminier was a stultified person. But a stultified person is neither lazy nor a fool. And we ourselves would be stultified if we didn't recognize in his theses the same art, the same intelligence, the same labor as those acts that transform wood, stone, or leather. It is only by recognizing Lerminier's *labor* that we can recognize the *intelligence* manifested in the most humble of works.

The poor village people who live outside of Grenoble work at making gloves; they are paid thirty cents a dozen. Since they became emancipated, they work hard at looking at, studying, and understanding a well-made glove. They will understand the meaning of all the *sentences*, all the *words* of the glove. They will end up speaking as well as the city women who earn seven francs a dozen. One has only to learn a language spoken with scissors, needle, and thread. It is merely a question (in human societies) of understanding and speaking a language.[21]

The material ideality of language refutes any opposition between the golden race and the iron race, any hierarchy—even an inverted one—between men devoted to manual work and men destined to the exercise of thought. Any work of language is understood and executed the same way. It is for this reason that the ignorant one can, as soon as he knows himself, verify his son's research in the book he doesn't know how to read: he doesn't know the materials he is working with, but if his son tells him how he goes to work at it, he will recognize if his son is doing research, because he knows what seeking, researching, is. He has only one thing to ask his son: to move words and sentences back and forth, as he himself moves his tools back and forth when he is seeking.

The book—*Télémaque* or any other—placed between two minds sums up the ideal community inscribed in the materiality of things. The book *is* the equality of intelligence. This is why the same philosophical commandment prescribed that the artisan do nothing but his own affair and condemned the democracy of the book. The Platonic philosopher-king favored the living word to the dead letter of the book—that thought-become-material at the disposition of men of substance, that discourse at once silent and too loquacious, wandering at random among those whose only business is thinking. The explicative privilege is only the small change of that interdiction. And the privilege that the Jacotot method gave to the book, to the manipulation of signs, to mnemotechnics, was the exact reversal of the hierarchy of minds that was designated in Plato by the critique of writing.[22] The book seals the new relation between two ignorant people who recognize each other from that point on as intelligent beings. And this new relation undoes the stultifying relation of intellectual instruction and moral education. Intervening in lieu of the disciplinary demands of education is the decision to emancipate that renders the father or mother capable of taking the ignorant schoolmaster's place—that place where the unconditional exigency of the will is incarnated. Unconditional exigency: the emancipatory father is not a simple good-natured pedagogue; he is an intractable master. The emancipatory commandment knows no compromises. It absolutely commands of a subject what it supposes it is capable of commanding of itself. The son will verify in the book the equality of intelligence in the same way that the father or mother will verify the radical nature of his research. The family unit is then no longer the place of a return that brings the artisan back to the consciousness of his incapacity. It is one of a new consciousness, of an overtaking of the self that extends each person's "own affair" to the point where it is part and parcel of the common reason enjoyed by all.

The Blind Man and His Dog

For it is indeed this that is verified: the principle of the equality of all speaking beings. By compelling his son's will, the father in a poor family verifies that his son has the same intelligence as he, that he seeks in the same way; and what the son, in turn, looks for in the book is the intelligence of the book's author, in order to verify that it proceeds in the same way as his own. That reciprocity is the heart of the emancipatory method, the principle of a new philosophy that the Founder, by joining together two Greek words, baptized "panecastic,"* because it looks for the *totality* of human intelligence in *each* intellectual manifestation. No doubt the landowner who sent his gardener to be trained at Louvain for the benefit of his own sons' instruction didn't understand this very well. There are no particular pedagogical performances to expect from an emancipated gardener or from the ignorant master in general. Essentially, what an emancipated person can do is be an emancipator: to give, not the key to knowledge, but the consciousness of what an intelligence can do when it considers itself equal to any other and considers any other equal to itself.

Emancipation is the consciousness of that equality, of that reciprocity that alone permits intelligence to be realized by verification. What stultifies the common people is not the lack of instruction, but the belief in the inferiority of their intelligence. And what stultifies the "inferiors" stultifies the "superiors" at the same time. For the only verified intelligence is the one that speaks to a fellow-man capable of verifying the equality of their intelligence. The superior mind condemns itself to never being understood by inferiors. He can only assure himself of his intelligence by disqualifying those who could show him

*From the Greek *pan*, everything, and *hekastos*, each: everything in each.—TRANS.

their recognition of it. Consider the scholar who *knows* that feminine minds are inferior to masculine minds; he spends the essential part of his life conversing with someone who cannot understand him: "What intimacy! What sweetness in the conversations of love! In the couple! In the family! He who is speaking is never sure of being understood. He has a mind and a heart, a great mind, a sensitive heart! But the corpse to which the social chain has attached him, alas!"[23] Will the admiration of his students and of the exterior world console him for this domestic disgrace? What worth is an inferior mind's judgment of a superior mind? "Tell a poet: I was very happy with your latest book. He will respond, pinching his lips: you give me *much* honor; that is to say, my dear fellow, I cannot be flattered by the commendation of so small an intelligence as yours."[24]

But the belief in intellectual inequality and in the superiority of one's own intelligence does not belong to scholars and distinguished poets alone. Its force comes from the fact that it embraces the entire population under the guise of humility. I can't, the ignorant one you are encouraging to teach himself declares; I am only a worker. Listen carefully to everything there is in that syllogism. First of all, "I can't" means "I don't want to; why would I make the effort?" Which also means: I undoubtedly could, for I am intelligent. But I am a worker: people like me can't; my neighbor can't. And what use would it be for me, since I have to deal with imbeciles?

So goes the belief in inequality. There is no superior mind that doesn't find an even more superior one to be lower to; no inferior mind that doesn't find a more inferior one to hold in contempt. The professorial gown of Louvain counts little in Paris. And the Parisian artisan *knows* how inferior provincial artisans are to him; these, in turn, know how backward peasants are. The day when those peasants think that they know things themselves, and that the Parisian professorial gown drapes a lamebrain, the loop will be closed. The universal superiority of inferiors will unite with the universal inferiority of superiors to create a world where no intelligence could recognize another as its equal. For reason is lost where one person speaks to another who is unable to reply to him. "There is no more beautiful spectacle, none more instructive, than the spectacle of a man speaking. But the listener must reserve the right to think about what he has just heard, and the speaker must engage with him in this. . . . The listener must thus verify if the speaker is actually within the bounds of reason, if he departs from it, if he returns to it. Without that authorized verification, necessitated by the very equality of intelligence, I see nothing in a conversation but a discourse between a blind man and his dog."[25]

The apology of the blind man speaking to his dog is the world of unequal intelligence's response to the fable of the blind leading the blind. We can see that it is a question of philosophy and humanity, not of recipes for children's pedagogy. Universal teaching is above all the universal verification of the similarity of what all the emancipated can do, all those who have decided to think of themselves as people just like everyone else.

Everything Is in Everything

Everything is in everything. The power of the tautology is that of equality, the power that searches for the finger of intelligence in every human work. This is the meaning of the exercise that astounded Baptiste Froussard, a progressive man and director of a school in Grenoble, who accompanied the two sons of the deputy Casimir Périer to Louvain. A member of the Society of Teaching Methods, Baptiste Froussard had already heard of universal teaching, and in Miss Marcellis's class, he recognized the exercises that the society's president, Jean de Lasteyrie, had described. He there saw young girls write compositions in fifteen minutes, some on the topic of "The Last Man," others on "The Exile's Return," creating, as the Founder assured him, pieces of literature "that *did not spoil the beauty of* the most beautiful pages of our best authors." It was an assertion that learned visitors had greeted with the deepest reservations. But Jacotot had found a way to convince them: since they evidently considered themselves to be among the best writers of their time, they had only to submit themselves to the same test and give the students the possibility of comparing. De Lasteyrie, who had lived through 1793, had lent himself willingly to the exercise. This had not been the case with Guigniaut, an envoy from the Ecole Normale in Paris who, though he was unable to see any significance in Calypso, had managed to see the unforgivable lack of a circumflex on *croître* in one of the compositions. Invited to the test, he arrived an hour late and was told to come back the next day. But that afternoon he caught the mail carriage for Paris, carrying in his baggage as damning evidence the shameful *i* deprived of a circumflex.

After reading the compositions, Baptiste Froussard sat in on classes of improvisation. This was an essential exercise in universal teaching: to learn to speak on any subject, off the cuff, with a beginning, a development, and an ending. Learning to improvise was first of all *learning to overcome oneself*, to overcome the pride that disguises itself as humility as an excuse for one's incapacity to speak in front of others—that is to say, one's refusal to submit oneself to their judgment. And after that it was learning to begin and to end, to make a *totality*, to close up language in a circle. Thus two students improvised with assurance on the topic of "The Atheist's Death," after which, to dissipate such sad thoughts, Jacotot asked another student to improvise on "The Flight of a Fly." Hilarity erupted in the classroom, but Jacotot was clear: this was not about laughing, it was about *speaking*. And the young student spoke for eight and a half minutes on this airy subject, saying charming things and making graceful, freshly imaginative connections.

Baptiste Froussard had also participated in a music lesson. Jacotot had asked him for fragments of French poetry, on which the students improvised melodies with accompaniments that they interpreted in a delightful manner. Baptiste Froussard came back to Miss Marcellis's several more times, assigning compositions himself on morals and metaphysics; all were performed with an admirable facility and talent. But the following exercise surprised him the most. One day, Jacotot addressed the students: "Young ladies, you know that in every human work there is art; in a steam engine as in a dress; in a work of literature as in a shoe. Well, you will now write me a composition on art in general, connecting your words, your expressions, your thoughts, to such and such passages from the assigned authors in a way that lets you justify or verify everything."[26]

Various books were brought to Baptiste Froussard, and he himself indicated to one student a passage from *Athalie*, to another a grammar chapter, to others a passage from Bossuet, chapters on geography, on division in Lacroix's arithmetic, and so on. He did not have to wait long for the results of this strange exercise on such barely comparable things. After a half hour, a new astonishment came over him when he heard the quality of the compositions just written beneath his nose, and the improvised commentaries that justified them. He particularly admired an explication of art done on the passage from *Athalie*, along with a justification or verification, which was comparable, in his opinion, to the most brilliant literary lesson he had ever heard.

That day, more than ever, Baptiste Froussard understood in what sense one can say that *everything is in everything*. He already knew that Jacotot was an astonishing pedagogue and he could guess at the quality of the students formed under his direction. But he returned home having understood one more thing: Miss Marcellis's students in Louvain had the same intelligence as the glovemakers in Grenoble, and even—this was more difficult to admit—as the glovemakers on the outskirts of Grenoble.

3 Reason Between Equals

We must look further into the reason for these effects: "We direct students based on an *opinion* about the equality of intelligence."

What is an opinion? An opinion, the explicators respond, is a feeling we form about facts we have superficially observed. Opinions grow especially in weak and common minds, and they are the opposite of science, which knows the true reasons for phenomena. If you like, we will teach you science.

Slow down. We grant you that an opinion is not a truth. But this is precisely what interests us: whoever does not know the truth is looking for it, and there are many encounters to make along the way. The only mistake would be to take our opinions for the truth. Admittedly, this happens all the time. But this is precisely the one way that we want to distinguish ourselves (we others, the followers of the madman): we think that our opinions are opinions and nothing more. We have seen certain facts. We believe that this could be the reason for it. We (and you may do the same) will perform some other experiments to verify the solidity of the opinion. Besides, it seems to us that this procedure is not completely new. Didn't physicists and chemists often proceed in this way? And we speak then about hypothesis, about the scientific method, in a respectful tone.

After all, respect means little to us. Let's limit ourselves to the facts: we have seen children and adults learn by themselves, without a master explicator, how to read, write, play music, and speak foreign languages. We believe these facts can be explained by the equality of intelligence. This is an opinion whose verification we pursue. It's true there is a difficulty in all this. Physicists and chemists isolate physical phenomena and relate them to other physical phenomena. They set themselves to reproducing the known effects by producing their supposed causes. Such a procedure is forbidden us. We can never say: take two equal minds and place them in such and such a condition. We know intelligence by its effects. But we cannot isolate it, measure it. We are reduced to multiplying the experiments inspired by that opinion. But we can never say: all intelligence is equal.

It's true. But our problem isn't proving that all intelligence is equal. It's seeing what can be done under that supposition. And for this, it's enough for us that the opinion be possible— that is, that no opposing truth be proved.

Of Brains and Leaves

Precisely, say the superior minds. The opposite fact is obvious. That intelligence is unequal is evident to everyone. First of all, in nature, no two beings are identical. Look at the leaves falling from the tree. They seem exactly the same to you. Look more closely and disabuse yourself. Among the thousands of leaves, there are no two alike. Individuality is the law of the world. And how could this law that applies to vegetation not apply *a fortiori* to this being so infinitely more elevated in the vital hierarchy that is human intelligence? *Therefore*, each intelligence is different. Second, there have always been, there always will be, there are everywhere, beings unequally gifted for intellectual things: scholars and ignorant ones, intelligent people and fools, open minds and closed minds. We know what is said on the subject: the difference in circumstances, social milieu, education . . . Well, let's do an experiment: let's take two children who come from the same milieu, raised in the same way. Let's take two brothers, put them in the same school, make them do the same exercises. And what will we see? One will do better than the other. There is therefore an intrinsic difference. And the difference results from this: one of the two is more intelligent, more gifted; he has more resources than the other. *Therefore*, you can clearly see that intelligence is unequal.

How to respond to this *evidence*? Let's begin at the beginning: with the leaves that superior minds are so fond of. We fully recognize that they are as different as people so minded could desire. We only ask: how does one move from the difference between leaves to the inequality of intelligence? Inequality is only a kind of difference, and it is not the one spoken about in the case of leaves. A leaf is a material thing while a mind is immaterial. How can one infer, without paralogism, the properties of the mind from the properties of matter?

It is true that this terrain is now occupied by some fierce adversaries: physiologists. The properties of the mind, according to the most radical of them, are in fact the properties of the human brain. Difference and inequality hold sway there just as in the configuration and functioning of all the other organs in the human body. The brain weighs this much, so intelligence is worth that much. Phrenologists and cranioscopists are busy with all this: this man, they tell us, has the skull of a genius; this other doesn't have a head for mathematics. Let's leave these *protuberants* to the examination of their protuberances and get down to the serious business. One can imagine a consequent materialism that would be concerned only with brains, and that could apply to them everything that is applied to material beings. And so, effectively, the propositions of intellectual emancipation would be nothing but the dreams of bizarre brains, stricken with a particular form of that old mental malady called melancholia. In this case, superior minds—that is to say, superior brains—would in fact have authority over inferior minds in the same way man has authority over animals. If this were simply the case, nobody would discuss the inequality of intelligence. Superior brains would not go to the unnecessary trouble of proving their superiority over inferior minds—incapable, by definition, of understanding them. They would be content to dominate them. And they wouldn't run into any obstacles: their intellectual superiority would be demonstrated by the fact of that domination, just like physical superiority. There would be no more need for laws, assemblies, and governments in the political order than there would be for teaching, explications, and academies in the intellectual order.

Such is not the case. We have governments and laws. We have superior minds that try to teach and convince inferior minds. What is even stranger, the apostles of the inequality of intelligence, in their immense majority, don't believe the physiologists and make fun of the phrenologists. The superiority they boast of can't be measured, they believe, by instruments. Materialism would be an easy explanation for their superiority, but they make a different case. Their superiority is spiritual. They are spiritualists, above all, because of their own good opinion of themselves. They believe in the immaterial and immortal soul. But how can something immaterial be susceptible to more or less? This is the superior minds' contradiction. They want an immortal soul, a mind distinct from matter, and they want different degrees of intelligence. But it's matter that makes differences. If one insists on inequality, one must accept the theory of cerebral loci; if one insists on the spiritual principle, one must say that it is the same intelligence that applies, in different circumstances, to different material objects. But the superior minds want neither a superiority that would be only material nor a spirituality that would make them the equals of their inferiors. They lay claim to the differences of materialists in the midst of the elevation that belongs to immateriality. They paint the cranioscopist's skulls with the innate gifts of intelligence.

And yet they know very well that the shoe pinches, and they also know they have to concede something to the inferiors, even if only provisionally. Here, then, is how they arrange things: there is in every man, they say, an immaterial soul. This soul permits even the most humble to know the great truths of good and evil, of conscience and duty, of God and judgment. In this we are all equal, and we will even concede that the humble often teach us in these matters. Let them be satisfied with this and not pretend to intellectual capacities that are the privilege— often dearly paid for—of those whose task is to watch over the general interests of society. And don't come back and tell us that these differences are purely social. Look instead at these two children, who come from the same milieu, taught by the same masters. One succeeds, the other doesn't. Therefore . . .

So be it! Let's look then at your children and your *therefore*. One succeeds better than the other, this is a *fact*. If he succeeds better, you say, this is *because* he is more intelligent. Here the explanation becomes obscure. Have you shown another *fact* that would be the cause of the first? If a physiologist found one of the brains to be narrower or lighter than the other, this would be a fact. He could *therefore-ize* deservedly. But you haven't shown us another fact. By saying "He is more intelligent," you have simply summed up the ideas that tell the story of the fact. You have given it a *name*. But the name of a fact is not its cause, only, at best, its metaphor. The first time you told the story of the fact by saying, "He succeeds better." In your retelling of it you used another name: "He is more intelligent." But there is no more in the second statement than in the first. "This man does better than the other because he is smarter. That means precisely: he does better because he does better. . . . This young man has more *resources*, they say. 'What is more resources?' I ask, and they start to tell me the story of the two children again; so *more resources*, I say to myself, means in French the set of facts I just heard; but that expression doesn't explain them at all."[1]

It's impossible, therefore, to break out of the circle. One must show the cause of the inequality, at the risk of borrowing it from the protuberants, or be reduced to merely stating a tautology. The inequality of intelligence explains the inequality of intellectual manifestations in the way the *virtus dormitiva* explains the effects of opium.

An Attentive Animal

We know that a justification of the equality of intelligence would be equally tautological. We will therefore try a different path: we will talk only about what we see; we will name facts without pretending to assign them causes. The first fact: "I see that man does things that other animals don't. I call this fact *mind, intelligence,* as I like; I explain nothing, I give a name to what I see."[2] I can also say that man is a reasonable animal. By that I am registering the fact that man has an articulated language that he uses to make words, figures, and comparisons for the purposes of communicating his thoughts to his fellow-men. Second, when I compare two individuals, "I see that in the first moments of life, they have absolutely the same intelligence, that is to say, they do exactly the same things, with the same goal, with the same intention. I say that these two humans have equal intelligence, and this phrase, *equal intelligence,* is shorthand for all the facts that I have observed watching two very young infants."

Later, I will see different facts. I will confirm that the two minds are no longer doing the same things, are not obtaining the same results. I could say, if I wanted to, that one's intelligence is more developed than the other's, so long as I know that, here again, I am only *recounting* a new fact. Nothing prevents me from making a supposition about all this. I will not say that the one's faculties are inferior to the other's. I will only suppose that the two faculties haven't been equally exercised. Nothing proves this to me with certainty. But nothing proves the opposite. It is enough for me to know that this lack of exercise is possible, and that many experiments attest to it. I will thus displace the tautology very slightly. I will not say that he has done less well because he is less intelligent. I will say that he has perhaps produced a poorer work because he has worked more poorly, that he has not seen well because he hasn't looked well. I will say that he has brought less attention to his work.

By this I may not have advanced very far, but far enough,

nevertheless, to break out of the circle. Attention is neither the skull surrounding the brain nor an occult quality. It is an immaterial fact in its principle, material in its effects: we have a thousand ways of verifying its presence, its absence, or its greater or lesser intensity. All the exercises of universal teaching tend toward this. In the end, the inequality of attention is a phenomenon whose possible causes are reasonably suggested to us through experiment. We know why young children direct so similar an intelligence to exploring their world and learning their language. Instinct and need drive them equally. They all have just about the same needs to satisfy, and they all want equally to enter human society enjoying all the advantages and rights of speaking beings. And for this, intelligence must not come to a standstill.

The child is surrounded by objects that speak to him, all at once, in different languages; he must study them separately and together; they have no relationship and often contradict each other. He can make nothing of all the idioms in which nature speaks to him—through his eyes, his touch, through all his senses—simultaneously. He must repeat often to remember so many absolutely arbitrary signs. . . . What great attention is necessary for all that!³

This giant step taken, the need becomes less imperious, the attention less constant, and the child gets used to learning through the eyes of others. Circumstances become diverse, and he develops the intellectual capacities as those circumstances demand. The same holds for the common people. It is useless to discuss whether their "lesser" intelligence is an effect of nature or an effect of society: they develop the intelligence that the needs and circumstances of their existence demand of them. There where need ceases, intelligence slumbers, unless some stronger will makes itself understood and says: continue; look at what you are doing and what you *can* do if you apply the same intelligence you have already made use of, by bringing to each thing the same attention, by not letting yourself stray from your path.

Let's sum up these observations and say: *man is a will served*

by an intelligence. Perhaps saying that wills are unequally demanding suffices to explain the differences in attention that
would perhaps suffice to explain the inequality of intellectual
performances.

Man is *a will served by an intelligence.* This formula is heir to
a long history. Summing up the thought of the great
eighteenth-century minds, the poet-philosopher Jean François
de Saint-Lambert affirmed: "Man is a living organization served
by an intelligence." The formula smacked of materialism, and
during the Restoration, the apostle of counterrevolution, the
Viscount de Bonald, strictly reversed it. "Man," he proclaimed,
"is an intelligence served by organs." But this reversal caused a
very ambiguous restoration of the intelligence. What the viscount disliked about the philosopher's formula was not that it
gave too small a part to human intelligence; he himself didn't
grant it much. What he disliked was the republican model of
a king at the service of a collective organization. What he
wanted to restore was the good hierarchical order: a king who
commands and subjects who obey. The sovereign intelligence,
for him, was certainly not that of the child or worker, tending
to the appropriation of a world of signs; it was the divine intelligence already inscribed in the codes given to man by the
divinity, in the very language that owed its origin neither to
nature nor to human art, but to the pure gift of God. Human
will's lot was to submit itself to that intelligence already manifested, inscribed in codes, in language as in social institutions.

Taking this stand brought with it a certain paradox. To en-
sure the triumph of social objectivity and the objectivity of language over the "individualist" philosophy of the Enlightenment, de Bonald had to take up in his turn the most "materialist" formulations of that same philosophy. In order to deny
any anteriority of thought over language, in order to forbid intelligence any right to search for a truth of its own, he had to
join up with those who had reduced mental operations to the
pure mechanism of material sensations and linguistic signs: to
the point of making fun of those monks on Mount Athos who,

contemplating their navels, believed themselves visited by divine inspiration.[4] Thus that co-naturality between linguistic signs and the ideas of understanding that the eighteenth century sought, and that the Ideologues worked at finding, found itself recuperated, reversed to favor the primacy of the established, in the framework of a theocratic and sociocratic vision of the intelligence. "Man," wrote the viscount, "thinks his speech before speaking his thought"—a materialist theory of language that does not allow us to ignore the pious thought that animates it: "The faithful and perpetual guardian of the sacred depository of the fundamental truths of the social order, society, considered in general, grants knowledge of all this to its children as they enter into the big family."[5]

In the face of these strong thoughts, an angry hand scratched on his copy these lines: "Compare all this scandalous verbiage with the oracle's response on the learned ignorance of Socrates." It isn't Joseph Jacotot's hand. It is the hand of de Bonald's colleague in the Chamber, the knight Maine de Biran, who, a little farther on, reverses the viscount's entire edifice in two lines: the anteriority of linguistic signs changes nothing for the preeminence of the intellectual act that, for every human infant, gives them meaning; "Man only learns to speak by linking ideas to the words he learns from his nurse."[6] At first glance this is an astonishing coincidence. At first it is difficult to see what the erstwhile lieutenant of Louis XVI's guard and the erstwhile army captain from Year I, the administrative squire and the professor from the central school, the deputy of the monarch's Chamber and the exiled revolutionary, could possibly have in common. At the most, we might think, the fact that both were twenty years old at the onset of the Revolution, that both left the tumult of Paris at twenty-five, and that both had meditated rather lengthily and at a distance on how much sense and virtue the old Socratic axiom might have had, or might have now, in the middle of so many upheavals. Jacotot understood the matter more in the manner of the moralists, Maine de Biran more metaphysically. Nevertheless, there remains a common vision that upholds the same affirmation of the primacy of thought over linguistic signs: the same balance sheet of the analytic and ideological tradition in which both had formed their thinking. Self-knowledge and the power of reason are no longer to be sought in the reciprocal transparency of linguistic signs and the ideas of understanding. The arbitrariness of the will—revolutionary and imperial—has now entirely taken over the promised land of well-made languages that yesterday's reason promised. Thus the certitude of thought withdraws beyond the transparencies of language—whether they be republican or theocratic. It bears on its own act, on that mental tension that precedes and orients any combination of signs. The divinity of the revolutionary and imperial era—the will—finds its rationality at the heart of that effort each puts into himself, that autodetermination of the mind as activity. Intelligence is attention and research before being a combination of ideas. Will is the power to be moved, to act by its *own* movement, before being an instance of choice.

A Will Served by an Intelligence

It is this fundamental turnaround that the new reversal of the definition of man records: man is a will served *by an intelligence*. Will is the rational power that must be delivered from the quarrels between the *idea-ists* and the *thing-ists*. It is also in this sense that the Cartesian equality of the *cogito* must be specified. In place of the thinking subject who only knows himself by withdrawing from all the senses and from all bodies, we have a new thinking subject who is aware of himself through the action he exerts on himself as on other bodies.

Here is how Jacotot, according to the principles of universal teaching, made his own *translation* of Descartes's famous analysis of the piece of wax:

I want to look and I see. I want to listen and I hear. I want to touch and my arm reaches out, wanders along the surfaces of objects or penetrates into their interior; my hand opens, develops, extends, closes up; my fingers spread out or move together by obeying my will. In that act of touching, I know only my will to touch. That will is neither my hand, nor my brain, nor my touching. That will is me, my soul, it is my power, it is my faculty. I feel that will, it is present in me, it is myself; as for the manner in which I am obeyed, that I don't feel, that I only know by its acts. . . . I consider ideation like touching. I have sensations when I like; I order my senses to bring them to me. I have ideas when I like; I order my intelligence to look for them, to feel. The hand and the intelligence are slaves, each with its own attributes. Man is a will served by an intelligence.[7]

I have ideas when I like. Descartes knew well the power of will over understanding. But he knew it precisely as the power of the false, as the cause of error: the haste to *affirm* when the idea isn't clear and distinct. The opposite must be said: it is the lack of will that causes intelligence to make mistakes. The mind's original sin is not haste, but distraction, absence. "To act without will or reflection does not produce an intellectual act. The effect that results from this cannot be classed among the products of intelligence, nor can it be compared to them. One can see neither more nor less action in inactivity; there is nothing. Idiocy is not a faculty; it is the absence or the slumber or the relaxation of [intelligence]."[8]

Intelligence's act is to see and to compare what has been seen. It sees at first by chance. It must seek to repeat, to create the conditions to re-see what it has seen, in order to see similar facts, in order to see facts that could be the cause of what it has seen. It must also form words, sentences, and figures, in order to tell others what it has seen. In short, the most frequent mode of exercising intelligence, much to the dissatisfaction of geniuses, is repetition. And repetition is boring. The first vice is laziness. It is easier to absent oneself, to half-see, to say what one hasn't seen, to say what one believes one sees. "Absent" sentences are formed in this way, the "therefores" that translate no mental adventure. "I can't" is one of these absent sentences. "I can't" is not the name of any fact. Nothing happens in the mind that corresponds to that assertion. Properly speaking, it doesn't *want* to say anything. Speech is thus filled or emptied of meaning depending on whether the will compels or relaxes the workings of the intelligence. Meaning is the work of the will. This is the secret of universal teaching. It is also the secret of those we call geniuses: the relentless work to bend the body to necessary habits, to compel the intelligence to new ideas, to new ways of expressing them; to redo on purpose what chance once produced, and to reverse unhappy circumstances into occasions for success:

This is true for orators as for children. The former are formed in assemblies as we are formed in life. . . . He who, by chance, made people laugh at his expense at the last session could learn to get a laugh whenever he wants to were he to study all the relations that led to the guffaws that so disconcerted him and made him close his mouth forever. Such was Demosthenes' debut. By making people laugh without meaning to, he learned how he could excite peals of laughter against Aeschines. But Demosthenes wasn't lazy. He couldn't be.[9]

Once more universal teaching proclaims: *an individual can do anything he wants.* But we must not mistake what wanting means. Universal teaching is not the key to success granted to the enterprising who explore the prodigious powers of the will. Nothing could be more opposed to the thought of emancipation than that advertising slogan. And the Founder became irritated when disciples opened their school under the slogan, "Whoever wants to is able to." The only slogan that had value was "The equality of intelligence." Universal teaching is not an expedient method. It is undoubtedly true that the ambitious and the conquerors gave ruthless illustration of it. Their passion was an inexhaustible source of ideas, and they quickly understood how to direct generals, scholars, or financiers faultlessly in sciences they themselves did not know. But what interests us is not this theatrical effect. What the ambitious gain in the way of intellectual power by not judging themselves inferior to anyone, they lose by judging themselves superior to everyone else. What interests us is the exploration of the powers of any man when he judges himself equal to everyone else and judges everyone else equal to him. By the will we mean that self-reflection by the reasonable being who knows himself in the act. It is this threshold of rationality, this consciousness of and esteem for the self as a reasonable being acting, that nourishes the movement of the intelligence. The reasonable being is first of all a being who knows his power, who doesn't lie to himself about it.

The Principle of Veracity

There are two fundamental lies: the one that proclaims, "I am telling the truth," and the one that states, "I cannot say." The reasonable being who reflects on himself knows the emptiness of these two propositions. The first fact is the impossibility of not knowing oneself. The individual cannot lie to himself; he can only forget himself. "I can't" is thus a sentence of self-forgetfulness, a sentence from which the reasonable individual has withdrawn. No evil genie can interpose himself between consciousness and its act. We must therefore reverse Socrates's adage. "No one is voluntarily bad," he said. We will say the opposite: "All blunders come from vice."[10] No one makes an error except by waywardness, that is to say, by laziness, by the desire to no longer listen to what a reasonable being owes himself. The principle of evil lies not in a mistaken knowledge of the good that is the purpose of action. It lies in unfaithfulness to oneself. "Know yourself" no longer means, in the Platonic manner, know where your good lies. It means come back to yourself, to what you know to be unmistakably in you. Your humility is nothing but the proud fear of stumbling in front of others. Stumbling is nothing; the wrong is in diverging from, leaving one's path, no longer paying attention to what one says, forgetting what one is. So follow *your* path.

This principle of veracity is at the heart of the emancipation experience. It is not the key to any science, but the privileged relation of each person to the truth, the one that puts him on his path, on his orbit as a seeker. It is the moral foundation of the power to know. This ethical foundation of the very ability to know is still a thought of its time, a fruit of the meditation on revolutionary and imperial experience. But the majority of the thinkers of the time understood it in the opposite way to Jacotot. For them, the truth that commands intellectual agreement was to be identified with the link that keeps men united. Truth is what brings together; error is rupture and solitude. Society, its institutions, the goal it pursues—these are what define the desire with which the individual must identify in order to reach a correct perception. Thus reasoned de Bonald the theocrat, and, after him, Philippe Buchez the socialist and Auguste Comte the positivist. The eclectics, with their common sense and their grand truths written in the heart of each person, be he philosopher or shoemaker, were less severe. But all were men of aggregation. And Jacotot departed from them on this point. One can say, if one likes, that truth brings together. But what brings *people* together, what unites them, is nonaggregation. Let's rid ourselves of the representation of the social cement that hardened the thinking minds of the postrevolutionary age. People are united because they are people, that is to say, *distant* beings. Language doesn't unite them. On the contrary, it is the arbitrariness of language that makes them try to communicate by forcing them to translate—but also puts them in a community of intelligence. Man is a being that knows very well when someone speaking doesn't know what he is talking about.

Truth doesn't bring people together at all. It is not given to us. It exists independently from us and does not submit to our piecemeal sentences. "Truth exists by itself; it is that which is and not that which is said. Saying depends on man, but the truth does not."[11] But for all that, truth is not foreign to us, and we are not exiled from its country. The experience of veracity attaches us to its absent center; it makes us circle around its foyer. First of all, we can see and indicate truths. Thus, "I taught what I didn't know" is a truth. It's the name of a fact that existed, that can be reproduced. As for the reason for this fact, that is for the moment an opinion, and it may always remain so. But with that opinion, we are circling around the truth, from fact to fact, relation to relation, sentence to sentence. What is essential is to avoid lying, not to say that we have seen something when we've kept our eyes closed, not to believe that something has been explained to us when it has only been named.

Thus, each one of us describes our parabola around the truth. No two orbits are alike. And this is why the explicators endanger our revolution.

These orbits of humanitarian conceptions rarely intersect and have only a few points in common. The jumbled lines that they describe never coincide without a disturbance that suspends liberty and, consequently, the use of the intelligence that follows from it. The student feels that, on his own, he wouldn't have followed the route he has just been led down; and he forgets that there are a thousand paths in intellectual space open to his will.[12]

This coincidence of orbits is what we have called stultification. And we understand why stultification is all the more profound, the more subtle, the less perceptible, the coincidence. This is why the Socratic method, apparently so close to universal teaching, represents the most formidable form of stultification. The Socratic method of interrogation that pretends to lead the student to his own knowledge is in fact the method of a riding-school master:

He orders turns, marches, and countermarches. As for him, during the training session he is relaxed and has the dignity of authority over the mind he directs. From detour to detour, the student's mind arrives at a finish that couldn't even be glimpsed at the starting line. He is surprised to touch it, he turns around, he sees his guide, the surprise turns into admiration, and that admiration stultifies him. The student feels that, alone and abandoned to himself, he would not have followed that route.[13]

No one has a relationship to the truth if he is not on his own orbit. But let no one, for all that, gloat about his singularity and go out, in his turn, to proclaim: *Amicus Plato, sed magis amica veritas!* That is a line from the theater. Aristotle, who said it, was doing nothing different from Plato. Like him, he was stating his opinions, he was telling the story of his intellectual adventures; on the way, he gathered a few truths. As for the truth, it doesn't rely on philosophers who say they are its friend: it is only friends with itself.

Reason and Language

Truth is not told. It is a whole, and language fragments it; it is necessary, and languages are arbitrary. It was this thesis on the arbitrariness of languages—even more than the proclamation of universal teaching—that made Jacotot's teaching scandalous. In 1818, in his very first course at Louvain, he took as his theme this question, inherited from the eighteenth century of Diderot and the Abbé Batteux: is "direct" construction, the one that places the noun before the verb and the attribute, the natural construction? And did French writers have the right to consider that construction a mark of their language's intellectual superiority? He decided negatively. With Diderot, he judged the "inverted" order to be as natural as the so-called natural order, if not more so; and he believed the language of sentiment preceded that of analysis. But he attacked above all the very idea of a natural order and the hierarchies it might entail. All languages were equally arbitrary. There was no language of intelligence, no language more universal than others.

The response didn't take long. In the next issue of *L'Observateur belge*, a literary journal out of Brussels, a young philosopher by the name of Van Meenen denounced the thesis as a theoretical warning to the oligarchy. Five years later, after the publication of *Langue maternelle*, a young lawyer close to Van Meenen who had taken Jacotot's courses and even published his notes, got angry in turn. In his *Essai sur le livre de Monsieur Jacotot*, Jean Sylvain Van de Weyer scolded this French professor who, after Bacon, Hobbes, Locke, Harris, Condillac, Dumarsais, Rousseau, Destutt de Tracy, and de Bonald, still dared to maintain that thought preceded language.

The position of these young and passionate contradictors is

easy to understand. They represented the young Belgium, patriotic, liberal, and French-speaking, in a state of intellectual insurrection against Flemish domination. To destroy the hierarchy of languages and the universality of the French language was, for them, to give the prize to the language of the Flemish oligarchy, the backward language of the less-civilized part of the population, but also the secret language of power. Following them, the *Courrier de la Meuse* attacked the Jacotot method for coming in the nick of time to impose at little cost the language and the civilization—in scare quotes—of the Flemish.

But there was more to it than this. These young defenders of the Belgian identity and the French intellectual landscape had read the Viscount de Bonald's *Recherches philosophiques*. They retained from it a fundamental idea: the analogy between the laws of language, the laws of society, and the laws of thought and their unity, in principle, in divine law. Undoubtedly they were departing from the viscount's philosophical and political message. They wanted a national and constitutional monarchy, and they wanted the mind to discover freely the great metaphysical, moral, and social truths inscribed by divinity on each person's heart. Their philosophical guiding light was a young philosopher in Paris named Victor Cousin. In the thesis of the arbitrariness of languages, they saw irrationality being introduced into the heart of communication, obstructing the discovery of the true course where the philosopher's meditation must commune with the common man's common sense. They saw in the lecturer from Louvain's paradox the perpetuation of the vice of those philosophers who "have frequently confused in their attacks, in the name of prejudices, both the deadly errors whose breeding ground they discovered not far from them and the fundamental truths that they attributed to the same origin. This is because the truth remained hidden from them in depths inaccessible to argumentation's scalpel and to the microscope of a verbose metaphysics, depths to which they had long ago given up descending, depths where one is guided by the clarity of good sense and a simple heart alone."[14]

The fact is that Jacotot did not want to *relearn* that kind of descent. He did not *hear* foolish sentences with good sense and a simple heart. He would have none of that fearful liberty guaranteed by the agreement of the laws of thought with the laws of language and those of society. Liberty is not guaranteed by any preestablished harmony. It is taken, it is won, it is lost, solely by each person's effort. And reason is not assured by being already written in language's constructions and the laws of the city. Language's laws have nothing to do with reason, and the laws of the city have everything to do with irrationality. If there is a divine law, thought itself, in its sustained truthfulness, alone bears witness to it. Man does not think *because* he speaks— this would precisely submit thought to the existing material order. Man thinks because he exists.

It remains that thought must be spoken, manifested in works, communicated to other thinking beings. This must be done by way of languages with arbitrary significations. One mustn't see in this an obstacle to communication. Only the lazy are afraid of the idea of arbitrariness and see in it reason's tomb. On the contrary. It is because there is no code given by divinity, no language of languages, that human intelligence employs all its art to making itself understood and to understanding what the neighboring intelligence is signifying. Thought is not told *in truth*; it is expressed *in veracity*. It is divided, it is told, it is translated for someone else, who will make of it another tale, another translation, on one condition: the will to communicate, the will to figure out what the other is thinking, and this under no guarantee beyond his narration, no universal dictionary to dictate what must be understood. Will figures out will. It is in this common effort that the definition of man as *a will served by an intelligence* takes on its meaning:

I think and I want to communicate my thought; immediately my intelligence artfully employs any signs whatsoever; it combines them, composes them, analyzes them; and an expression, an image, a material fact, emerges that will henceforth be for me the portrait of a thought, that is to say, of an immaterial fact. It will recall my thought for me, and I will think of it each time I see its portrait. I can thus converse with myself when I like. And then, one day, I find myself face to face with another man; I repeat, in his presence, my gestures and my words and, if he likes, he will figure me out. . . .

But one cannot reach an agreement through words about the meaning of words. One man wants to speak, the other wants to figure it out, and that's that. From this agreement of wills there results a thought visible to two men at the same time. At first it exists immaterially for one of them; then he says it to himself, he gives form to it with his eyes or his ears, and finally he wants that form, that material being, to reproduce for another man the same primitive thought. These creations or, if you will, these metamorphoses are the effect of two wills helping each other out. Thought thus becomes speech, and then that speech or that word becomes thought again; an idea becomes matter, and that matter becomes an idea—and all this is the effect of the will. Thoughts fly from one mind to another on the wings of words. Each word is sent off with the intention of carrying just one thought, but, unknown to the one speaking and almost in spite of him, that speech, that word, that larva, is made fruitful by the listener's will; and the representative of a monad becomes the center of a sphere of ideas radiating out in all directions, such that the speaker has actually said an infinity of things beyond what he wanted to say; he has formed the body of an idea with ink, and the matter destined to mysteriously envelop a solitary immaterial being actually contains a whole world of those beings, those thoughts.[15]

Perhaps we can now better understand the reason for universal teaching's marvels: the strengths it puts into play are simply those of any situation of communication between two reasonable beings. The relation between two ignorant people confronting the book they don't know how to read is simply a radical form of the effort one brings every minute to translating and counter-translating thoughts into words and words into thoughts. The will that presides over the operation is not a magician's secret spell. It is the desire to understand and to be understood without which no man would ever give meaning to the materialities of language. Understanding must be understood in its true sense: not the derisive power to unveil things, but the power of translation that makes one speaker confront another. It is the same power that allows the "ignorant" one to find the secret of the "mute" book. Despite what the *Phaedrus* teaches us, there are not two kinds of discourses, one of which could be deprived of the power to "help itself" and be condemned to stupidly repeat the same thing. All words, written or spoken, are a translation that only takes on meaning in the counter-translation, in the invention of the possible causes of the sound heard or of the written trace: the will to figure out that applies itself to all indices, in order to know what one reasonable animal has to say to what it considers the soul of another reasonable animal.

Perhaps we can now better understand the scandal that made *telling the story* and *figuring out* the two master operations of the intelligence. Undoubtedly the truth-tellers and the superior minds know other ways of transforming mind into matter and matter into mind. It's understandable that they would keep these from the profane. For the latter, as for any reasonable being, there is then only this movement of speech that is at once a known distance, sustained by truth, and the consciousness of humanity: the wish to communicate with others and to verify one's similarity with them. "Man is condemned to have feelings and to be silent or, if he wishes to speak, to speak indefinitely since he must always rectify by adding or taking away from what he just said. . . . [For whenever someone says something about it], he must hasten to add: it isn't that. And since the rectification is no more complete than the first statement, we arrive at, in this flux and reflux, a kind of perpetual improvisation."[16]

We know that improvisation is one of the canonical exercises of universal teaching. But it is first of all the exercise of our intelligence's leading virtue: the poetic virtue. The impossibility of our *saying* the truth, even when we *feel* it, makes us speak as poets, makes us tell the story of our mind's adventures and verify that they are understood by other adventurers, makes us communicate our feelings and see them shared by other feeling beings. Improvisation is the exercise by which the human being knows himself and is confirmed in his nature as a reasonable man, that is to say, as an animal "who makes words, figures, and comparisons, to tell the story of what he thinks to those like him."[17] The virtue of our intelligence is less in knowing than in doing. "Knowing is nothing, *doing* is everything." But this doing is fundamentally an act of communication. And, for that, "*speaking* is the best proof of the capacity to do whatever it is."[18] In the act of speaking, man doesn't transmit his knowledge, he makes poetry; he translates and invites others to do the same. He communicates as an *artisan*: as a person who handles words like tools. Man communicates with man through the works of his hands just as through the words of his speech: "When man acts on matter, the body's adventures become the story of the mind's adventures."[19] And the artisan's emancipation is first the regaining of that story, the consciousness that one's material activity is of the nature of discourse. He communicates as a *poet*: as a being who believes his thought communicable, his emotions sharable. That is why speech and the conception of all works as discourse are, according to universal teaching's logic, a prerequisite to any learning. The artisan must speak about his works in order to be emancipated; the student must speak about the art he wants to learn. "Speaking about human works is the way to know human art."[20]

Me Too, I'm a Painter!

From this follows the strange method by which the Founder, among his other follies, taught drawing and painting. We begin by asking the student to talk about what he is going to represent—let's say a drawing to copy. It would be dangerous to give the child explanations of the measures he must take before beginning his work. We know the reason for this: the risk that the child will sense in this, his inability. We will thus trust in the child's will to imitate. But we are going to *verify* that will. A few days before putting a pencil in his hand, we will give him the drawing to look at, and we will ask him to talk about it.

Perhaps he will only say a few things at first—for example, "The head is pretty." But we will repeat the exercise; we will show him the same head and ask him to look again and speak again, at the risk of repeating what he already said. Thus he will become more attentive, more aware of his ability and capable of imitating. We know the reason for this effect, something completely different from visual memorization and manual training. What the child has *verified* by this exercise is that painting is a language, that the drawing he has been asked to imitate *speaks* to him. Later on, we will put him in front of a painting and ask him to improvise on the *unity of feeling* present, for example, in that painting by Poussin of the burial of Phocion. The connoisseur will undoubtedly be shocked by this, won't he? How could you pretend to know that this is what Poussin wanted to put in his painting? And what does this hypothetical discourse have to do with Poussin's pictorial art and with the one the student is supposed to acquire?

We will answer that we don't pretend to know what Poussin wanted to do. We are simply trying to imagine what he might have wanted to do. We thus verify that all *wanting to do* is a *wanting to say* and that this wanting to say is addressed to any reasonable being. In short, we verify that the *ut poesis pictura* the artists of the Renaissance had claimed by reversing Horace's adage is not knowledge reserved solely for artists: painting, like sculpture, engraving, or any other art, is a language that can be understood and spoken by whoever knows the language. As far as art goes, "I can't" translates easily, we know, into "that says nothing to me." The verification of the "unity of feeling," that is to say, of the meaning of the painting, will thus be the means of emancipation for the person who "doesn't know how" to paint, the exact equivalent to the verification-by-book of the equality of intelligence.

Undoubtedly, there's a great distance from this to making masterpieces. The visitors who appreciated the literary compositions of Jacotot's students often made a wry face at their paintings and drawings. But it's not a matter of making great painters; it's a matter of making the emancipated: people capable of saying, "me too, I'm a painter," a statement that contains nothing in the way of pride, only the reasonable feeling of power that belongs to any reasonable being. "There is no pride in saying out loud: Me too, I'm a painter! Pride consists in saying softly to others: You neither, you aren't a painter."[21] "Me too, I'm a painter" means: me too, I have a soul, I have feelings to communicate to my fellow-men. Universal teaching's method is identical to its morals:

We say in universal teaching that every man who has a soul was born with a soul. In universal teaching we believe that man feels pleasure and pain, and that it is only up to him to know when, how, and by what set of circumstances he felt this pleasure or pain. . . . What is more, man knows that there are other beings who resemble him and to whom he could communicate his feelings, provided that he places them in the circumstances to which he owes his pains and his pleasures. As soon as he knows what moved him, he can practice moving others if he studies the choice and use of the means of communication. It's a language he has to learn.[22]

The Poets' Lesson

One must *learn*. All men hold in common the ability to feel pleasure and pain. But this resemblance is for each only a probability to be verified. And it can be verified only by the long path of the dissimilar. I must verify the reason for my thought, the humanity of my feelings, but I can do it only by making them venture forth into the forest of signs that by themselves don't want to say anything, don't correspond with that thought or that feeling. Since Boileau, it has been said that if something is well conceived, it will be clearly articulated. This sentence is meaningless. Like all sentences that surreptitiously slip from thought to matter, it expresses no intellectual adventure. Conceiving well is a resource of any reasonable person. Articulating well is an artisan's work that supposes the exercise of the tools of language. It is true that reasonable man can do anything. But

he must still learn the proper language for each of the things he
wants to do: to make shoes, machines, or poems. Consider, for
example, the affectionate mother who sees her son come back
from a long war. The shock she feels robs her of speech. But
"the long embraces, the hugs of a love anxious at the very moment of happiness, a love that seems to fear a new separation;
the eyes in which joy shines in the middle of tears; the mouth
that smiles in order to serve as the interpreter of the equivocal
language of tears; the kisses, the looks, the attitude, the sighs,
even the silence,"²³—all that *improvisation* in short—is this not
the most eloquent of poems? You feel the emotion of it. But try
to communicate it. The instantaneousness of these ideas and
feelings that contradict each other and are infinitely nuanced—
this must be transmitted, made to voyage in the wilds of words
and sentences. And the way to do that hasn't been invented. For
then we would have to suppose a third level in between the individuality of that thought and common language. Would this
be still another language, and how would its inventor be understood? We are left with learning, with finding the tools of that
expression in books. Not in grammarians' books: they know
nothing of this voyage. Not in orators' books: these don't seek
to be *figured out*; they want to be *listened to*. They don't want to
say anything; they want to command—to join minds, submit
wills, force action. One must learn near those who have worked
in the gap between feeling and expression, between the silent
language of emotion and the arbitrariness of the spoken tongue,
near those who have tried to give voice to the silent dialogue the
soul has with itself, who have gambled all their credibility on
the bet of the similarity of minds.

Let's learn, then, near those poets who have been adorned
with the title genius. It is they who will betray to us the secret
of that imposing word. The secret of genius is that of universal
teaching: learning, repeating, imitating, translating, taking
apart, putting back together. In the nineteenth century, it is
true certain geniuses began to boast of superhuman inspiration.
But the classics, those geniuses, didn't drink out of the same

cup. Racine wasn't ashamed of being what he was: a worker. He learned Euripides and Vergil by heart, *like a parrot*. He tried translating them, broke down their expressions, recomposed them in another way. He knew that being a poet meant translating two times over: translating into French verse a mother's sadness, a queen's wrath, or a lover's rage was also translating how Euripides or Vergil translated them. From Euripides' *Hippolytus*, one had to translate not only Phèdre—that's understood—but also Athalie and Josabeth. For Racine had no illusions about what he was doing. He didn't think he had a better understanding of human sentiments than his listeners. "If Racine knew a mother's heart better than I, he would be wasting his time telling me what he read in it; I would not recognize his observations in my memories, and I would not be moved. This great poet presumes the opposite; all his work, all his care, all his revisions, are performed in the hope that everything will be understood by his readers exactly as he understands it himself."[24] Like all creators, Racine instinctively applied the method, that is to say, the moral, of universal teaching. He knew that there are no men of *great thoughts*, only men of *great expressions*. He knew that all the power of the poem is concentrated in two acts: translation and counter-translation. He knew the limits of translation and the powers of counter-translation. He knew that the poem, in a sense, is always the absence of another poem: that silent poem that a mother's tenderness or a lover's rage improvises. In a few rare effects, the first approaches the second to the point of imitating it, as in Corneille, in one or three syllables: "Me," or better, "That he die!" For the rest, the poet is suspended in the counter-translation the listener will do of it. It is the counter-translation that will produce the poem's emotion; it is the "sphere of ideas radiating forth" that will reanimate the words. All of the poet's effort, all his work, is to create that aura around each word, each expression. It is for this reason that he analyzes, dissects, translates others' expressions, that he tirelessly erases and corrects his own. He strives to say everything, knowing that everything cannot be said, but that it is the unconditional tension of the translator that opens the possibility of the other tension, the other will: language does not allow everything to be said, and "I must have recourse to my own genius, to all men's genius, to figure out what Racine meant, what he would say as a man, what he says when he is not speaking, what he cannot say since he is only a poet."[25]

This is the true modesty of the "genius," that is to say, of the emancipated artist: he employs all his art, all his power, to show us his poem as the absence of another that he credits us with knowing as well as he. "We believe ourselves to be Racine, and we are right." This belief has nothing to do with any charlatan's pretension. It in no way implies that our verse is as good as Racine's, or that it soon will be. It means first that we understand what Racine has to tell us, that his thoughts are not different from ours, and that his expressions are only achieved by our counter-translation. We know first *through him* that we are people like him. And we also know through him the power of a language that makes us know this via the arbitrariness of signs. We know our "equality" with Racine thanks to the fruit of Racine's work. His genius lies in having worked by the principle of the equality of intelligence, in having not believed himself superior to those he was speaking to, in having even worked for those who predicted that he would fade like a season. It is left to us to verify that equality, to conquer that power through our own work. This does not mean making tragedies equal to Racine's; it means, rather, employing as much attention, as much artistic research as he, to recounting how we feel and to making others feel it, despite the arbitrariness of language or the resistance of all matter to the work of our hands. The artist's emancipatory lesson, opposed on every count to the professor's stultifying lesson, is this: each one of us is an artist to the extent that he carries out a double process; he is not content to be a mere journeyman but wants to make all work a means of expression, and he is not content to feel something but tries to impart it to others. The artist needs equality as the explicator needs inequality. And he therefore designs the model of a reasonable society where the very thing that is outside of reason—matter, linguistic signs—is traversed by reasonable will: that of telling the story and making others feel the ways in which we are similar to them.

The Community of Equals

We can thus dream of a society of the emancipated that would be a society of artists. Such a society would repudiate the division between those who know and those who don't, between those who possess or don't possess the property of intelligence. It would only know minds in action: people who do, who speak about what they are doing, and who thus transform all their works into ways of demonstrating the humanity that is in them as in everyone. Such people would know that no one is born with more intelligence than his neighbor, that the superiority that someone might manifest is only the fruit of as tenacious an application to working with words as another might show to working with tools; that the inferiority of someone else is the consequence of circumstances that didn't compel him to seek harder. In short, they would know that the perfection someone directs toward his own art is no more than the particular application of the power common to all reasonable beings, the one that each person feels when he withdraws into that privacy of consciousness where lying makes no sense. They would know that man's dignity is independent of his position, that "man is not born to a particular position, but is meant to be happy in himself, independently of what fate brings,"[26] and that the reflection of feeling that shines in the eyes of a wife, a son, or a dear friend presents to the gaze of a sensitive enough soul adequate satisfaction.

Such people would not be occupied creating phalansteries where vocations would correspond to passions, communities of equals, economic organizations harmoniously distributing functions and resources. To unite humankind, there is no better

link than this identical intelligence in everyone. It is this that
is the just measure of similarity, igniting that gentle penchant
of the heart that leads us to help each other and love each other.
It is this that gives someone the means of measuring the extent
of the services that he can hope for from his fellow-man and of
devising ways to show him his appreciation. But let's not talk
like utilitarians. The principal service that man can expect from
man depends on that faculty of intercommunicating their pleasure and pain, hopes and fears, in order to be moved recipro-
cally: "If men didn't have the faculty, an equal faculty, they
would soon become strangers to each other; they would scatter
at random throughout the globe and societies would be dis-
solved. . . . The exercise of that power is at once the sweetest
of our pleasures and the most demanding of our needs."[27]

We scarcely have to ask what these wise people would have
in the way of laws, magistrates, assemblies, and tribunals.
People who obey the dictates of reason have no need of laws and
magistrates. The Stoics knew that already: virtue that knows
itself, the virtue of knowing oneself, is the guiding power of
all other virtues. But we ourselves know that reason is not the
privilege of the wise. There are no madmen except those who
insist on inequality and domination, those who want to be
right. Reason begins when discourses organized with the goal
of being right cease, begins where equality is recognized: not
an equality decreed by law or force, not a passively received
equality, but an equality in act, verified, at each step by those
marchers who, in their constant attention to themselves and in
their endless revolving around the truth, find the right sentences to make themselves understood by others.

We must therefore reverse the critics' questions. How, they
ask, is a thing like the equality of intelligence thinkable? And
how could this opinion be established without disrupting the
social order? We must ask the opposite question: how is intelligence possible without equality? Intelligence is not a power
of understanding based on comparing knowledge with its object. It is the power to make oneself understood through an-

other's verification. And only an equal understands an equal. *Equality* and *intelligence* are synonymous terms, exactly like *reason* and *will*. This synonymy on which each man's intellectual capacity is based is also what makes society, in general, possible. The equality of intelligence is the common bond of humankind, the necessary and sufficient condition for a society of men to exist. "If men considered themselves equal, the constitution would soon be completed."[28] It is true that we don't know that men are equal. We are saying that they *might* be. This is our opinion, and we are trying, along with those who think as we do, to verify it. But we know that this *might* is the very thing that makes a society of humans possible.

4] The Society of Contempt

But there is no such thing as a *possible* society. There is only the society that exists. We were getting lost in our dreams, but here comes someone knocking at the door. It's the envoy from the Minister of Public Instruction, who has come to call to Monsieur Jacotot's attention the royal decree setting out the conditions for establishing a school in the kingdom. It's the officer from the Military School of Delft assigned to bring order to the strange Ecole Normale Militaire in Louvain. It's the messenger bringing the last issue of *Annales Academiae Lovaniensis*, containing the *oratio* of our colleague Franciscus Josephus Dumbeck, who sounds the charge against universal teaching, the new corrupter of youth:

Since education embraces the totality of the people and its first virtue resides in unitary harmony, a perverse method can destroy that unity and split the city into opposing camps. . . . Let us rid the country of this madness. Guided by the love of beauty and of literature, studious young people must not only attempt to flee laziness as the most serious of evils; they must also cling to that Decency, that Modesty, celebrated by all antiquity with divine honors. Only then will they be citizens of the elite, defenders of law, masters of virtue, interpreters of the divine commandments, upholders of the country, of the honor of an entire race. . . . And you too, Royal Majesty, must listen! For it is to you that the care of your subjects has been confided, especially at that tender age. It is a sacred duty to annihilate teachers of this kind, to suppress schools of darkness![1]

The kingdom of the Netherlands is a small state, but it is civilized just like a big one. Public authority holds the education of young people and the harmony of citizens among its most privileged concerns. Opening a school is not granted to just anyone—not to someone without a certificate, but especially not to someone who boasts of teaching what he doesn't know, and of exciting people against the schoolmasters, assistant schoolmasters, rectors, inspectors, commissioners, and ministers who hold to a higher idea of their duties to youth and to science. *Absit hic a nostra patria furor!* Or, in our own words, "Stultification, rearing its ugly head, cries out to me: go back, you mad innovator! The species you want to take away from me is attached to me by indissoluble chains. I am what was, what is, and what shall be on earth, as long as souls inhabit bodies of clay. Today, less than ever, can you hope for success. They believe in progress, and their opinions are solidly hinged on this; I laugh at your efforts; they will not budge."[2]

The Law of Gravity

We were getting lost watching thinking minds orbiting around the truth. But matter's movements obey other laws: those of attraction and gravity. All bodies mindlessly hurl themselves toward the center. We have said that nothing can be induced about minds from leaves, about the immaterial from the material. Intelligence does not follow the laws of matter. But this much is true for each individual's intelligence taken separately: it is indivisible, without community, without division. It cannot, therefore, belong to any group, for then it would no longer belong to the individual. We must therefore conclude that intelligence is only in individuals, that it is not in their *union*.

Intelligence is in each intellectual unity; the union of these unities is necessarily inert and without intelligence. . . . In the cooperation of two intellectual molecules called men, there are two minds; they are of the same nature, but it isn't one, unique intelligence that presides over this cooperation. In matter, a unique force, gravity, animates mass and molecules; but in the class of intellectual beings, intelligence directs individuals alone; their union is subject to the laws of matter.[3]

We have seen reasonable individuals crossing over the bounds of linguistic materiality in order to signify their thought to one another. But this interchange is possible only on the basis of the inverted relation that submits the union of intelligences to the laws of any grouping, those of matter. Here we have the material hinge of stultification: immaterial minds cannot be *linked together* except by making them submit to the laws of matter. The free orbit of each intelligence around the absent star of the truth, the distant flight of free communication on the wings of the word, is found to be thwarted, driven off course by universal gravitation toward the center of the material universe. Everything happens as though the intelligence lived in a double world. And maybe we should give some credit to the Manichean hypothesis: Manicheanism saw disorder in creation, and explained it by the meeting of two kinds of intelligence. It's not simply that there is a principle of good and a principle of evil. More profoundly, it's that two intelligent principles don't make *one* intelligent creation. At the moment when the Viscount de Bonald proclaimed the restoration of divine intelligence, manager of language and of human society, some men of progress were tempted to revive, in opposition, the hypotheses of the heretics and the Manicheans. They compared the powers of intelligence at work in scholars and inventors with the sophistries and disorders of deliberative assemblies, and willingly saw in this the action of two antagonistic principles. This is how it was for Jeremy Bentham and his disciple James Mill, witnesses of the madness of English conservative assemblies, as well as for Joseph Jacotot, witness of the madness of French revolutionary assemblies.

But let's not blame the absent divinity too quickly, and let's not let the actors in these madnesses completely off the hook. Perhaps we should simplify the hypothesis: divinity is one; it is man who is double. Divinity gave man a will and an intelligence with which to respond to the needs of his existence. These were given to individuals, not to the species. The species doesn't need one or the other. It doesn't need to watch over its preservation. It is individuals who preserve the species. It is they alone who need a reasonable will to guide freely the intelligence placed at their service. On the other hand, we cannot expect reason from the social group. It is because it is, and that's that. And it can only be arbitrary. A case has been made, we know, for its foundation in nature: the case for the inequality of intelligence. In this case, we saw, the social order would be natural. "Human laws, the laws of convention, would be useless for preserving it. Obedience to these laws would no longer be a duty or a virtue; it would derive from the intellectual superiority of the qadis and the janissaries, and such groups would rule on the same grounds as man rules over animals."[4]

We can see clearly that it is not like this. Therefore convention alone can reign in the social order. But is convention necessarily unreasonable? We have seen that the arbitrariness of language proved nothing against the rationality of communication. We could thus imagine another hypothesis: one where each of the individual wills that make up the human species would be reasonable. In this case, everything would happen as though the human species were itself reasonable. The wills would become harmonious, and human groups would follow a straight line, without jostling, without deviation, without error. But how can we reconcile such uniformity with the liberty of individual wills, each of which can use or not use reason whenever it pleases? "The moment of reason for one corpuscle is not the same as for its neighboring atoms. In any given moment there is always reason, distraction, passion, calm, attention, wakefulness, sleep, relaxation, progress—in all directions. *Therefore*, in a given moment, a corporation, a nation, a species, a type, is at once reasonable and irrational, and the result does not depend at all on the will of the group. *Therefore*, it is precisely because each man is free that a union of men is not."[5]

The Founder emphasized his "therefores": this is not an incontestable truth he is developing for us; it's a supposition, an adventure of his mind that he recounts starting from the facts he has observed. We have already seen that the mind, the alliance between will and intelligence, knows two fundamental modalities: attention and distraction. There need only be distraction for intelligence to give way, for it to be overcome by the gravitation of matter. Thus certain philosophers and theologians explain original sin as a simple distraction. In this sense we can say with them that evil is only an absence. But we also know that this absence is also a refusal. The distracted person *doesn't see why* he should pay attention. Distraction is laziness first, the desire to retire from effort. But laziness itself isn't the torpor of the flesh; it is the act of the mind underestimating its own power. Reasonable communication is based on the equality between self-esteem and the esteem of others. It works toward the continuous verification of that equality. Contempt is the principle behind the laziness that causes intelligence to plummet into material gravity. This contempt tries to pass itself off as modesty: I can't, says the ignorant one who wants to withdraw from the task of learning. We know through experience what that modesty means. Self-contempt is always contempt for others. I can't, says the student who doesn't want to submit his improvisation to his peers' judgment. I don't understand your method, someone says; I'm incompetent; I don't understand anything about it. You quickly understand what he means: "This isn't common sense, since *I don't understand it*; a man like me!"[6] So it goes at any age and at all levels of society.

These beings who pretend to be slighted by nature only want pretexts to dispense with some study they don't like, some exercise that is distasteful to them. Do you want to be convinced? Wait a minute, let them speak, hear them out. After the rhetorical precaution issued by this modest character, who lacks, he says, a poetic mind, do you hear what solidity of judgment he attributes to himself? What perspicacity distinguishes him! Nothing escapes him; if you let him continue, the metamorphosis is at last complete, and now the modesty is transformed into pride. We can find examples of this in every village as in every city. Another's superiority in some realm is recognized so that one's own superiority in some other realm will be recognized, and it isn't difficult to see, at the end of the speech, that our superiority always ends up being, in our eyes, the superior superiority.[7]

Inequality's Passion

We can thus assign a unique passion as the cause of the distraction by which intelligence consents to matter's destiny: contempt, inequality's passion. It isn't love of wealth or possessions that perverts the will; it's the need to think under the sign of inequality. Hobbes composed a more *attentive* poem on this subject than Rousseau; social evil does not come from the first person who bethought himself to say, "This is mine." It comes from the first person who bethought himself to say, "You are not my equal." Inequality is not the consequence of anything; it is a primitive passion. Or, more exactly, it has no other cause than equality. Inegalitarian passion is equality's vertigo, laziness in face of the infinite task equality demands, fear in face of what a reasonable being owes to himself. It is easier to *compare* oneself, to establish social exchange as that swapmeet of glory and contempt where each person receives a superiority in exchange for the inferiority he confesses to. Thus the equality of reasonable beings vacillates within social inequality. To remain within the metaphor of our cosmology, we will say that it is the passion of *preponderance* that has subjected free will to the material system of weightiness, that has caused the mind to plummet into the blind world of gravitation. It is inegalitarian irrationality that makes the individual renounce himself, renounce the incommensurable immateriality of his essence, and that engenders aggregation as a fact and as the reigning collective fiction. The love of domination requires people to protect themselves from each other in the heart of a conventional order that cannot be reasonable, since it is made up of nothing but the irrationality of each—that submission to another's laws that the desire to be superior to him fatally entails. "The creation of our imagination that we call humankind is made up of our individual madnesses without partaking of our individual wisdom."[8]

So let's not blame blind necessity or the ill fate of being a soul enclosed in a body of clay and subjected to the evil divinity of matter. There is no evil divinity, no fatal mass, no radical evil. There is only this passion or fiction of inequality that brings its own consequences. That is why social submission can be described in two apparently contradictory manners. We could say that the social order is subject to an irrevocable material necessity, that it moves, like the planets, by eternal laws that no individual can change. But we could just as easily say that it is only a fiction. Type, species, corporation—nothing of the sort has any reality. Only individual humans are real; they alone have a will and an intelligence, and the totality of the order that subjects them to humankind, to social laws and to diverse authorities, is only a creation of the imagination. These two ways of speaking amount to the same thing: it's the irrationality of each person that endlessly creates and recreates this overwhelming mass, this absurd fiction, to which each citizen must subject his will, but from which each man also has the means of withdrawing his intelligence.

What we do, what we say in court, as in the tribunal, as in war, is regulated by suppositions. Everything is a fiction: only the consciousness and reason that each of us has is invariable. The social state, moreover, is founded on these principles. If man obeyed reason, then laws, magistrates, and all that would be unneeded; but passions carry him along: he revolts, he is punished in quite a humiliating manner. Each of us finds himself forced to look for the support of another against someone else. . . . It is obvious that from the moment men form society for the purpose of protecting themselves against each other, this reciprocal need announces an alienation of reason that promises no reasonable result. What better can society do than to chain us to that unhappy condition to which we ourselves are devoted![9]

Thus the social world is not simply the world of non-reason; it is that of irrationality, which is to say, of an activity of the perverted will, possessed by inequality's passion. In *linking* one person or group to another by *comparison*, individuals continually reproduce this irrationality, this stultification that institutions codify and explicators solidify in their brains. This production of irrationality is a work at which individuals employ as much art, as much intelligence, as they would for the reasonable communication of their minds' works. Except that this work is a work of grief. War is the law of the social order. But by the term "war," let us not think here of any fatal clash of material forces, any unleashing of hordes dominated by bestial instincts. War, like all human works, is first an act of words. But these words reject the halo of ideas radiating from a counter-translator representing another intelligence and another discourse. The will no longer attempts to figure out and to be figured out. It makes its goal the other's silence, the absence of reply, the plummeting of minds into the material aggregation of consent.

The perverted will doesn't stop using intelligence, but its use is based on a fundamental *distraction*. It habituates intelligence into only seeing what contributes to preponderance, what serves to cancel out the other's intelligence. The universe of social irrationality is made up of wills served by intelligences. But each of these wills charges itself with destroying another will by preventing another intelligence from seeing. And we know that this result isn't difficult to obtain. One need only play the radical exteriority of the linguistic order against the exteriority of reason. The reasonable will, guided by its distant link with the truth and by its desire to speak with those like it, controls that exteriority, regains it through the force of attention. The distracted will, detoured from the road of equality, uses it in the opposite way, in the rhetorical mode, to hasten the aggregation of minds, their plummet into the universe of material attraction.

Rhetorical Madness

This is the power of rhetoric: the art of *reasoning* that tries to annihilate reason under the guise of reason. Once the English and French revolutions put the power of deliberative assemblies back at the center of political life, curious minds revived Plato's and Aristotle's grand inquiry into the power of the false that imitates the power of the truth. That is why, in 1816, the Genevan Etienne Dumont translated his friend Jeremy Bentham's *Treatise on Parliamentary Sophistries* into French. Jacotot doesn't mention this work. But we can feel its influence in the parts of the *Langue maternelle* devoted to rhetoric. Like Bentham, Jacotot puts the irrationality of deliberative assemblies at the center of his analysis. The vocabulary he uses to talk about them is close to Dumont's. And his analysis of false modesty recalls Bentham's chapter on the argument *ad verecundiam*.[10] But if both exposed the machinery of the same comedy, they differed radically in their outlook and in the moral they drew from it. Bentham's polemic was against the English conservative assemblies. He demonstrated the ravages of the well-cloaked authoritarian arguments that the beneficiaries of the existing order employed to oppose any progressive reform. He denounced the allegories that hypostasize the existing order, the words that throw a veil, pleasant or sinister as needed, over things, the sophistries that serve to associate any proposition for reform with the specter of anarchy. For him these sophistries are explained by the play of interest, their success by the intellectual weakness of the voting public and the state of servitude under which it is kept by authority. This is to say that disinterested and free-thinking, rational men can combat them successfully. And Dumont, less impetuous than his friend, insisted on the reasonable hope that assimilates the progress of moral institutions to that of the physical sciences. "Aren't there in morals as in physics, errors that philosophy has caused to disappear? . . . It is possible to discredit false arguments to the point that they no longer dare show themselves. Do I need any other proof for this than the doctrine, famous for so long, even in England, of the divine *right* of kings and of the *passive obedience* of the people?"[11]

So the principles of disinterested reason can be set against the sophistries of private interest in the theater of politics itself. This supposes the culture of a reason that pits a precision of terms against the metaphors, analogies, and allegories that have invaded the political field, creating the field with words, forging it from absurd reasonings with the help of these words, and thereby casting a veil of prejudice over the truth. Thus, "the figurative expression of a body-politic has produced a great number of false and extravagant ideas. An analogy, founded solely on this metaphor, has furnished a foundation for pretended arguments, and poetry has invaded the dominion of reason."[12] Against this figurative language, this religious or poetic language that allows irrational interest to drape itself in all kinds of disguises, it is possible to oppose a true language in which words exactly overlap ideas.

Jacotot took exception to such optimism. There is no language of reason. There is only a control of reason over the intention to speak. Poetic language that knows itself as such doesn't contradict reason. On the contrary, it reminds each speaking subject not to take the narrative of his mind's adventures for the voice of truth. Every speaking subject is the poet of himself and of things. Perversion is produced when the poem is given as something other than a poem, when it wants to be imposed as truth, when it wants to force action. Rhetoric is perverted poetry. This means that it too falls in the class of fiction. Metaphor is bound up with the original resignation of reason. The body politic is a fiction, but a fiction is not a figurative expression to which an exact definition of the social group could be opposed. There is really a logic of bodies from which no one, *as a political subject*, can withdraw. Man can be reasonable, the citizen cannot. There is no reasonable rhetoric, no reasonable political discourse.

Rhetoric, it is said, has war as its principle. One doesn't seek comprehension in it, only the annihilation of the adverse will. Rhetoric is speech in revolt against the poetic condition of the speaking being. It speaks in order to silence. *You will speak no longer, you will think no longer, you will do this*: that is its program. Its efficacity is regulated by its own suspension. Reason commands us to speak always; rhetorical irrationality speaks only to bring about the moment of silence—the moment of the act, we say willingly, in homage to the person who makes action out of words. But this moment is instead much more one of the lack of an act, of absent intelligence, of subjugated will, of men subjected to the unique law of gravity.

The orator's successes are the work of the moment; he does away with a decree the way someone storms a fortification. . . . The length of the pauses, the literary order, elegance, all the qualities of style, are not what lends merit to this kind of discourse. It is a sentence, a word, sometimes an accent, a gesture, that awakened the sleeping people and elevated the mass that tends always to fall back down under its own weight. As long as Manilius could point to the Capitol, the gesture saved him. As soon as Phocion could seize the moment to speak a sentence, Demosthenes was conquered. Mirabeau understood this; he directed movements, compelled an easing up, through sentences and words; queried on three points, he replied, he even discussed them at length in an effort to change, little by little, peoples' minds; then he suddenly departed from parliamentary habits and closed the discussion in one word. However long the orator's discourse, it is never the length, it is never the exposition, that grants victory: the least skilled antagonist will meet well-rounded sentences with well-rounded sentences, exposition with exposition. The orator is whoever triumphs; it is whoever pronounced the word, the sentence that tipped the balance.[13]

We see that this superiority judges itself: it is the superiority of gravity. The superior man who tips the balance will always be he who best foresees when and how it will tip. He who bends others best is he who bends best himself. By submitting to his own irrationality, he causes the masses' irrationality to triumph. Whoever wants to be the people's master is forced to be their slave: so Socrates had taught Alcibiades, as he had Callicles before him. Alcibiades might be amused by the foolish face of a shoemaker glimpsed in his workshop and expound on the stupidity of *those people*; the philosopher would be content to reply to him: "Why aren't you more at ease when you have to speak in front of those people?"[14]

The Superior Inferiors

"That was the case long ago," the superior mind, habituated to the serious speech of voters' assemblies, will say. This was true of the demagogic assemblies drawn from the scum of the people who turned to and fro like a weathervane from Demosthenes to Aeschines, and from Aeschines back to Demosthenes. Let's look at this more closely. The *stupidity* that made the Athenian people turn sometimes to Aeschines, sometimes to Demosthenes, had a very precise content. What made them surrender alternatively to the one or the other was not their ignorance or their versatility. It was that this speaker or that one, at a particular moment, knew best how to incarnate the specific stupidity of the Athenian people: the feeling of its obvious superiority over the imbecile people of Thebes. In short, what moved the masses was the same thing that animates superior minds, the same thing that makes society turn on itself from one age to the next: the sentiment of the inequality of intelligence, the sentiment that distinguishes superior minds only at the price of confusing them with universal belief. Even today, what is it that allows the thinker to scorn the worker's intelligence if not the worker's contempt for the peasant—like the peasant's for his wife, the wife's for his neighbor's wife, and so on unto infinity. Social irrationality finds its formula in what could be called the paradox of the "superior inferiors": each person is subservient to the one he represents to himself as inferior, subservient to the law of the masses by his very pretension to distinguish himself from them.

Don't try to find an alternative to these demagogic assemblies in the reasonable serenity of assemblies made up of grave and respectable notables. Wherever people join together on the basis of their superiority over others, they give themselves over to the law of material masses. An oligarchical assembly, a congress of "honest people" or of "capable ones," will thus obey the brute law of matter much more certainly than a democratic assembly. "A senate has a determined pace and direction that it cannot itself change, and the orator that propels it down its own road and follows in its steps, always wins out over the others."[15] Appius Claudius, absolutely opposed to taking any instructions from the plebeians, was the senatorial orator par excellence, because he understood better than any other the inflexibility of the movement that pushed the leaders of the Roman elite in "their" direction. His rhetorical machine, the machine of superior men, seized a unique day: the day when the plebeians gathered on the Aventine. It would have taken a madman (that is to say, a reasonable man) to save things on that day, someone capable of an extravagance impossible and incomprehensible for an Appius Claudius: going to listen to the plebeians, presuming that their mouths emitted a language and not just noises; speaking to them, supposing they had the intelligence to understand the words of superior minds; in short, considering them equally reasonable beings.

The parable of the Aventine recalls the paradox of the inegalitarian fiction: social inequality is unthinkable, impossible, except on the basis of the primary equality of intelligence. Inequality cannot think itself. Even Socrates advised Callicles in vain that to break out of the master-slave circle he must learn that true equality is proportion, thus joining the circle of those who think of justice in terms of geometry. Wherever there is caste, the "superior" gives up his reason to the inferior's law. An assembly of philosophers is an inert body that moves on the axis of its own irrationality, the irrationality of everyone. Inegalitarian society tries in vain to understand itself, to give itself a natural foundation. It's precisely because there is no natural reason for domination that convention commands and commands absolutely. Those who explain domination by superiority fall into the old aporia: the superior ceases being that when he ceases dominating. The Duke of Lévis, academician and peer of France, worried about the social consequences of the Jacotot system: if one proclaimed the equality of intelligence, why would wives still obey their husbands, and the administrated their administrators? If the duke hadn't been *distracted*, like all superior minds, he would have noticed that it was his system, that of the inequality of intelligence, that was subversive of the social order. If authority depends on intellectual superiority, what will happen on the day when an administrated person, himself also convinced of the inequality of intelligence, thinks his prefect is an imbecile? Won't it be necessary to test ministers and prefects, burgermeisters and office heads, to verify their superiority? And how will we be sure that some imbecile, whose shortcomings when recognized would lead to citizens' disobedience, might not slip in among them?

Only the partisans of the equality of intelligence can understand this: if the qadi makes his slaves obey him, the white man his blacks, it is because he is neither superior nor inferior to them in intelligence. If circumstances and conventions separate and make hierarchies among men, if they create authority and force obedience, it is because they alone are capable of doing that. "It's precisely because we are all equal by nature that we must all be unequal by circumstances."[16] Equality remains the only reason for inequality. "Society exists only through distinctions, and nature presents only equalities. It is in fact impossible for equality to last for a long time; but even when it is destroyed, it remains the only reasonable explanation for conventional distinctions."[17]

The equality of intelligence does even more for inequality: it proves that the overturning of the existing order would be just as irrational as the order itself. "If someone asks me, What do you think of the organization of human societies? I would respond: This spectacle seems against nature. Nothing is in its place, since there are different places for beings that aren't different. And if human reason is called on to change the order, it would have to recognize its incapacity to do so. Order for order, places for places, differences for differences, there are no reasonable motives for change."[18]

The Philosopher-King and the Sovereign People

Thus equality alone remains capable of explaining an inequality that the inegalitarians will always be powerless to imagine. Reasonable man knows the reason for his irrationality as a citizen. But he knows it at the same time to be insurmountable. He is alone in knowing the circle of inequality. But as a citizen, he himself is enclosed in it. "There is only one reason; yet it hasn't organized the social order. So, happiness could not lie therein."[19] Philosophers are undoubtedly right to denounce the functionaries who try to rationalize the existing order. That order has no reason. But they deceive themselves by pursuing the idea of a social order that would finally be rational. The two extreme and symmetrical poles of that pretension are known: the old Platonic dream of the philosopher-king and the modern dream of the people's sovereignty. Undoubtedly a king can be a philosopher just like any other man. As the head, a king has at his disposal his ministers' reason, who have their bureau heads' reason, who in turn have everybody's reason. It's true that he is not dependent on his superiors—only on his inferiors. But the philosopher-king or the kingly philosopher takes part in society; and society imposes its laws, its superiorities, and its explanatory corporations on him, as it does on everyone.

This is also why the other pole of the philosophical dream, the people's sovereignty, is no sounder. For that sovereignty, presented as an ideal to be realized or a principle to be imposed, has always existed. And history resounds with the names of those kings who lost their throne for having ignored it: not one of them reigns except by the weight given him by the masses. The philosophers are indignant. The people, they say, cannot part with its sovereignty. We will answer that perhaps it *can't*, but that it has always done so since the beginning of the world. "Kings don't make peoples; they would try in vain to do so. But peoples can make leaders, and they have always wanted to do so."[20] The people is alienated from its leader exactly like the leader from his people. This reciprocal subjugation is the very principle of the political fiction whose origin lies in the alienation of reason by the passion of inequality. The philosophers' paralogism is to assume a people of *men*. But this is a contradictory expression, an impossible being. There are only peoples of citizens, people who have given up their reason to the inegalitarian fiction.

Let's not confuse this alienation with another. We aren't saying that the citizen is the ideal man, the inhabitant of an egalitarian political heaven that masks the reality of the inequality between concrete individuals. We are saying the opposite: that there is no equality except between men, that is to say, between individuals who regard each other only as reasonable beings. The citizen, on the contrary, the inhabitant of the political fiction, is man fallen into the land of inequality.

Reasonable man knows, therefore, that there is no political science, no politics of truth. Truth settles no conflict in the public place. It speaks to man only in the solitude of his conscience. It withdraws the moment that conflict erupts between two consciences. Whoever hopes to meet up with it must know, in any case, that it travels alone, without any retinue. Political opinions, on the other hand, never fail to give themselves the most imposing retinue: "Brotherhood or Death," they say; or, when their turns come, "Legitimacy or Death," "Oligarchy or Death," etc. "The first term varies but the second is always expressed or understood on the flags, the banners of all opinions. On the right, we read *The Sovereignty of A or Death*. On the left it's *The Sovereignty of B or Death*. Death is never missing; I even know philosophers who say, *Suppression of the Death Penalty or Death*."[21] As for truth, it isn't given any sanction; it doesn't associate with death. Following Pascal, let's say: we have always already found the means of giving justice to force, but we aren't close to finding the way to give force to justice. The very project doesn't make sense. A force is a force. It can be reasonable to make use of it. But it is irrational to want to render it reasonable.

How to Rave Reasonably

So it remains to the reasonable man to submit to the madness of being a citizen, while trying to safeguard his reason. Philosophers believe they have found the way: no *passive* obedience, they say, no duties without rights! But this is speaking from *distraction*. There is nothing, there will never be anything, in the idea of duty that implies rights. Whoever is alienated is absolutely alienated. To suppose anything else is a poor ruse of vanity that has no other effect than to rationalize alienation and to trick the one who pretends otherwise. Reasonable man will not be taken in by these tricks. He will know that the social order has nothing better to offer him than the superiority of order over disorder. "Any sort of order, so long as it cannot be troubled: that has characterized social organizations since the beginning of the world."[22] Keeping a monopoly on legitimate violence is still the proven best way to limit violence and allow reason some asylum where it can be freely practiced. Reasonable man thus does not consider himself above the law. Were he to attribute this superiority to himself, he would plummet into the destiny of those inferior superiors who constitute the human species and maintain its irrationality. He will consider the social order a mystery situated beyond reason's power, the work of a superior reason that requires the partial sacrifice of his own. He will submit himself as citizen to that which the irrationality of governments requires, refusing only to adopt the reasons given by it. He will not, for all that, abdicate his reason. He will bring it back to its first principle. Reasonable will, we have seen, is first of all the art of conquering oneself. Reason will preserve itself faithfully by controlling its own sacrifice. Reasonable man will be *virtuous*. He will partially give away his reason at the command of irrationality, in order to maintain the threshold of rationality that is the capacity to conquer oneself. Thus reason will always maintain an impenetrable stronghold in the middle of irrationality.

Social irrationality is war in its two aspects: the battlefield and the tribunal. The battlefield is the true portrait of society, the consequence produced exactly and integrally by the opinion on which it is founded.

When two men meet each other, they are polite as though they believed each other equal in intelligence; but if one of them is found deep in the middle of the other's country, there is no longer as much ceremony: he abuses his force like his reason: everything about the intruder denotes a barbarian origin; he is treated without ceremony like an idiot. His pronunciation causes peals of laughter; the awkwardness of his gestures, everything about him, announces the bastard species to which he belongs: they are a heavy people, we are light and frivolous; they are coarse, we are proud and high-minded. In general, one people believes itself in good faith to be superior to another people; and when a little passion is thrown in, war erupts: as many people as possible are killed, on both sides, like insects being crushed. The more killed, the more glory. One is paid so much per head; a cross is demanded for a burned village, a great ribbon if it's a big city; and this traffic in blood is called love of country. . . . It is in the name of country that you attack neighboring peoples like savage beasts; and if you were asked what your country is, you would all cut each other's throats before agreeing on the matter.[23]

And yet, says a chorus of philosophers and the common conscience, we must make distinctions. There are unjust wars, wars of conquest that the madness of domination demands; and there are just wars, those where we defend the ground of our country under attack. The former artilleryman Joseph Jacotot must have known this, he who had defended his endangered country in 1792 and who, in 1815, opposed with all his parliamentarian strength the King's return in the hands of the invaders. But it was precisely his experience that allowed him to notice that the morality of the thing was completely different from what it had seemed at first. The defender of the country under attack does as a citizen what he would not do as a man. He doesn't have to sacrifice his reason to virtue. For reason requires the reasonable animal to do what he can to preserve himself as a living being. Reason, in this case, is reconciled with war, and egoism with virtue. There is thus no particular merit in all this. On the other hand, he who obeys the orders of the conquering country, if he is reasonable, meritoriously sacrifices his reason to society's mystery. He needs far more virtue to preserve his interior fortress and to know, when duty is done, how to return to nature, to reconvert into the virtue of free thought the self-mastery he invested in being obedient as a citizen.

But for all this, war between armies is still reason's least difficult test. Reason is content to control its own suspension. It suffices for it to dominate itself as it obeys the voice of an authority that has enough power to make itself unequivocally heard by everyone. Much more perilous is action in those places where authority is yet to be established in the midst of contradictory passions: in assemblies deliberating law, in tribunals judging how it is to be applied. These places present reason with the same sort of mystery to which one can only bow down. In the middle of passion's brouhaha and irrationality's sophistries, the balance tips; law makes *its* voice heard, a voice that must be obeyed like that of a general. But this mystery requires the reasonable man's participation. It invites reason not onto the terrain of sacrifice but onto terrain that it assures it is its own, that of *reasoning*. And yet the reasonable man knows it is only a matter of combat: only the laws of war prevail. Success depends on the fighter's address and force, not his reason. This is why passion reigns here through its weapon, rhetoric. Rhetoric, we know, has nothing to do with reason. But is the opposite true? Doesn't reason have anything to do with rhetoric? Isn't it, in general, the speaking being's control of himself that permits him to make, in any domain, an *artistic* work? Reason would not be itself if it didn't grant the power to speak in the assembly as in any other place. Reason is the power to learn all languages. It will thus learn the language of the assembly and the tribunal. It will learn to rave.

So we must first side with Aristotle and against Plato: it is shameful for the reasonable man to get beaten in a tribunal, shameful for Socrates to have lost the battle and his life to Meletus and Anytus. The language of Anytus and Meletus, the orator's language, must be learned. And it is learned like other languages, more easily, even, than the others, for its vocabulary and syntax are enclosed in a tight circle. The "everything is in everything" slogan applies better here than in any other study. Thus *something* must be learned—a speech by Mirabeau, for example—and the rest will follow. This rhetoric that required so much work for the students of the Old Master is a game for us: "We know everything in advance; everything is in our books: only the names must be changed."[24]

But we also know that the bombast of sentences and stylistic ornament are not the quintessence of oratorical art. Their function is not to persuade minds but to *distract* them. What carries the decree—just as against a fortification—is assault, words, the decisive gesture. An assembly's fate is often decided by the audacious person who, to stifle discussion, is the first to cry out "voice vote!" So let us also learn, we too, the art of crying out "voice vote!" at the right moment. Let us not say this isn't worthy of us and of reason. Reason doesn't need us; it's we who need it. Our so-called dignity is only laziness and cowardice, similar to that of the proud child who doesn't want to improvise in front of his peers. In a little while, perhaps, we will also cry out "voice vote!" But we will shout it out along with the band of cowards who are echoing the winning orator—he who will have dared what we were too lazy to do.

Is it, then, a matter of making universal teaching into a school of political cynicism, reviving the sophistries Bentham denounced? Whoever wants to understand this lesson of the *reasonable man raving* must rather compare it with that of the *ignorant schoolmaster*. It is a question of verifying, in all cases, reason's power, of always seeing what can be done with it, what it can do to remain active in the very heart of extreme irrationality. The *reasonable man raving*, enclosed in the circle of social madness, shows that the individual's reason never ceases to exercise its power. In the closed field of the passions—exercises of the distracted will—it must be shown that attentive will can always do as much—and more than—what the passions can do. The queen of the passions can do better than they who are her slaves. "The most seductive sophistry, the one with the most verisimilitude, will always be the work of the person who knows best what a sophistry is. He who knows the right way departs from it when necessary, as much as is necessary, and never too much. No matter what superiority passion grants us, it can itself be dazzled, since it is a passion. Reason sees everything as it is: it shows, it hides, as much as it deems suitable, never more nor less."[25] This is a lesson not in ruse but in constancy. He who knows how to remain true to himself in the middle of irrationality will triumph over the passions of others exactly as he triumphs over his own. "Everything is done by the passions, I know; but everything, even follies, would be much better done by reason. This is the unique principle of Universal Teaching."[26]

Are we then that far from Socrates? He too taught, in the *Phaedrus* as in *The Republic*, that the philosopher will tell the good lie, the one that is exactly necessary and sufficient, because he alone knows what lying is. The whole difference for us is precisely in this: we suppose that everyone knows what lying is. It is even by this that we defined the reasonable being, by his incapacity to lie *to himself*. We are thus not speaking at all about the wise man's privilege, but about the power of reasonable people. And this power depends on an *opinion*, that of the equality of intelligence. This is the opinion that was missing in Socrates, and that Aristotle couldn't correct. The very superiority that allows the philosopher to locate the tiny difference that fools every time dissuades him from speaking to the "companions of slavery."[27] Socrates did not want to make a speech to please the people, to seduce the "ungainly animal." He didn't want to study the art of the sycophants Anytus and Meletus. He thought, and practically everyone praised him for it, that this would decay his own philosophy. But the basis for his opinion is this: Anytus and Meletus are imbecilic sycophants; thus, there is no art in their speeches, only recipes; there is nothing to be learned from them. Yet the speeches of Anytus and Meletus were a manifestation of the human intelligence *like* those of Socrates. We won't say they were as good. We will say that they derived from the same intelligence. Socrates, the "ignorant one," thought himself superior to the tribunal orators; he was too lazy to learn their art; he consented to the world's irrationality. Why did he act like this? For the same reason that defeated Laius, Oedipus, and all the tragic heroes: he believed in the Delphic oracle; he thought that he was the elect of the divinity, that she had sent him a personal message. He shared the madness of superior beings: the belief in genius. A divinely inspired being doesn't learn Anytus's speeches, doesn't repeat them, doesn't try, when he needs to, to appropriate their art. It is thus that the Anytuses become masters in the social order.

But, one may still ask, wouldn't they be anyway? What good is triumphing in the forum if one already knows that nothing can change the social order? What good is it for reasonable individuals—or the emancipated, if you will—to save their lives and safeguard their reason, if they can do nothing to change society and are reduced to the sad advantage of raving better than the madmen?

The Speech on the Aventine

Let's reply first of all that the worst is never certain, since, in a given social order, it's possible for all individuals to be reasonable. Society as such will never be reasonable, but it could experience the miracle of reasonable moments arising not in the coincidence of intelligences—that would be stultification—but in the reciprocal recognition of reasonable wills. When the

Senate raved, we joined Appius Claudius's chorus. That was the way to get it over with most quickly, to get to the scene on the Aventine sooner. It's Menenius Agrippa who is speaking now. And the details of what he is telling the plebeians matter little. The essential is that he is speaking to them, and they are listening to him; that they are speaking to him and he hears them. He speaks to them about legs and arms and stomachs, and that's perhaps not very flattering. But what he imparts to them is their equality as speaking beings, their capacity to understand as soon as they recognize themselves as equally marked by the sign of intelligence. He tells them they are the stomachs—this derives from the art learned by studying and repeating, by breaking apart and putting back together others' speeches; let's say, anachronistically, that it derives from intellectual emancipation. But he speaks to them as men, and, in so doing, makes them into men: this derives from intellectual emancipation. At the moment when society threatens to be shattered by its own madness, reason performs a saving social action by exerting the totality of its own power, that of the recognized equality of intellectual beings.

For this moment of civil war undone, this moment of the reconquered, victorious power of reason, it was worth having saved his reason for so long, and apparently so futilely, by learning from Appius Claudius the art of raving better than he. There is a life to reason that can remain faithful to itself within social irrationality, and it can have an effect. This is what we must work toward. Whoever knows how, for the good of the cause, to compose, with equal attention, the diatribes of an Appius Claudius or the fables of a Menenius Agrippa is a student of universal teaching. Whoever recognizes, along with Menenius Agrippa, that every man is born to understand what any other man has to say to him knows intellectual emancipation.

These happy encounters amount to little, say the impatient or the self-satisfied. And the Aventine is old history. But precisely at the same time, other voices, very different voices, make themselves heard, to affirm that the Aventine is the beginning of our history: that of the self-knowledge that makes yesterday's plebeians and today's proletarians capable of doing anything a man can do. In Paris, another eccentric dreamer, Pierre-Simon Ballanche, tells the story of the Aventine in his own way, and reads in it the same law proclaimed: that of the equality of speaking beings, of the power acquired by those who recognize themselves marked with the sign of intelligence and thus become capable of marking a name in heaven. And he announces this strange prophecy: "Roman history, as it has appeared to us up till now, after having in part ordered our destiny, after having entered, in one form, into the composition of our social life, our customs, our opinions, our laws, comes now, in a different form, to order our new thoughts, those that must enter into the composition of our future social life."[28] In the workshops of Paris or Lyon, a few dreaming minds hear this story and recount it in their turn and in their manner.

Undoubtedly this prophecy of a new era is a daydream. But this is not a daydream: one can always, at the very heart of inegalitarian madness, verify the equality of intelligence, and that verification has an effect. The victory on the Aventine is very real. And undoubtedly it isn't where we think it is. The tribunes the plebeians won would rave just like the others. But that every plebeian felt himself a man, believed himself capable, believed his son and any other person capable, of exercising the prerogatives of intelligence—this is not *nothing*. There cannot be a class of the emancipated, an assembly or a society of the emancipated. But any individual can always, at any moment, be emancipated and emancipate someone else, announce to others the *practice* and add to the number of people who know themselves as such and who no longer play the comedy of the inferior superiors. A society, a people, a state, will always be irrational. But one can multiply within these bodies the number of people who, as individuals, will make use of reason, and who, as citizens, will know how to seek the art of raving as reasonably as possible.

It can thus be said, and it must be said: "If each family did what I am saying, the nation would soon be emancipated, not with the emancipation *given* by scholars, by their explications *at the level of* the people's intelligence, but with the emancipation seized, even against the scholars, when one teaches oneself."[29]

5] The Emancipator and His Monkey

The duty of Joseph Jacotot's disciples is thus simple. They must announce to everyone, in all places and all circumstances, the news, the practice: one can teach what one doesn't know. A poor and ignorant father can thus begin educating his children: *something must be learned and all the rest related to it, on this principle: everyone is of equal intelligence.*

They must announce this principle and devote themselves to its verification: speak to the destitute person, make him talk about what he is and what he knows; show him how to instruct his child; copy the prayer that the child knows by heart; give him the first volume of *Télémaque* and have him learn it by heart; respond to the demand of those who want to learn from the master of universal teaching *what he doesn't know*; finally, use all possible means of convincing the ignorant one of his power. A disciple in Grenoble couldn't persuade a poor and elderly woman to learn to read and write. He paid her to get her consent. She learned in five months, and now she is emancipating her grandchildren.[1]

This is what must be done, all the while aware that a knowledge of *Télémaque* or of any other thing is, in itself, irrelevant. The problem is not to create scholars. It is to raise up those who believe themselves inferior in intelligence, to make them leave the swamp where they are stagnating—not the swamp of ignorance, but the swamp of self-contempt, of contempt *in and of itself* for the reasonable creature. It is to make emancipated and emancipating men.

Emancipatory Method and Social Method

Universal teaching shouldn't be placed on the program of reformist parties, nor should intellectual emancipation be inscribed on the banners of sedition. Only a man can emancipate a man. Only an individual can be reasonable, and only with his own reason. There are a hundred ways to instruct, and learning also takes place at the stultifiers' school; a professor is a *thing*, less easily handled than a book, undoubtedly, but he can be *learned*: he can be observed, imitated, dissected, put back together; his person, available for observation, can be tested. One always learns when listening to someone speaking. A professor is neither more nor *less* intelligent than another man, and he generally presents a great quantity of facts for the researcher's observation. But there is only one way to emancipate. And no party or government, no army, school, or institution, will ever emancipate a single person.

This is not at all a metaphysical proposition. The experiment was performed in Louvain, under the patronage of His Majesty, the King of the Netherlands. We know that the King was enlightened. His son, Prince Frederick, was taken with philosophy. Responsible for the army, he wanted it modern and educated, like the Prussian army. He was interested in Jacotot, suffered because of the disgrace the academic authorities of Louvain held him in, and wanted to do something for him, and for the Dutch army as well. At that time the army was a privileged terrain for trying out reformist ideas and new pedagogies. The Prince so conceived it, and persuaded his father to create a military school in Louvain and to confide the pedagogical mission to Jacotot.

This was a good intention but a poisoned gift: Jacotot was a *master*, not the head of an institution. His method was designed to form emancipated men, not military instructors, or indeed servants of any kind of social speciality. Let's understand this well: an emancipated man can just as well be a military instructor as a locksmith or a lawyer. But universal teaching cannot, without being *spoiled*, specialize in the production of a set kind of social actor—especially if these social actors are instructors of a body of men, military or otherwise. Universal teaching belongs to families, and the best that an enlightened ruler can do for its propagation is to use his authority to protect the free circulation of the service. An enlightened king can certainly *establish* universal teaching when and where he pleases, but such an establishment would not endure, for the human *animal* belongs to the old method. The experiment could undoubtedly be attempted, for the glory of the ruler. It would obviously fail, but there are instructive failures. Only one guarantee was required: the absolute concentration of power, the social scene swept clean of all its intermediaries to give free rein to just one couple, the King and the philosopher. This, then, was necessary: first, to get rid of all the advisers of the old method in the conventional manner of civilized countries, that is to say, by giving them all a promotion; second, to suppress all intermediaries other than those chosen by the philosopher; and third, to give all power to the philosopher:

They would do what I said, everything I said, nothing but what I said, and the responsibility would weigh entirely on me. I would ask for nothing; on the contrary, the intermediaries would ask me what was to be done, and how it was to be done, everything to be proposed to the King. I would be regarded not as an employed functionary, but as a philosopher whose consultations were needed. Finally, the establishment of universal teaching would be considered, for the time being, the first and foremost of all the affairs in the Kingdom.[2]

These are conditions that no civilized monarchy could accommodate, especially for a sure failure. Nevertheless, the King insisted on the experiment, and Jacotot, as grateful guest, accepted a bastard trial of cohabitation with a commission of military instruction, under the authority of the commander in charge at Louvain. The school was created on this basis in March

1827, and the students, at first bewildered to hear through an interpreter that their professor had nothing to teach them, must have found some benefit in it, since at the end of their regular term, they petitioned to have their stay at school prolonged so they might learn languages, history, geography, mathematics, physics, chemistry, topographical drawing, and fortification by the universal method. But the master wasn't satisfied with this *spoiled* universal teaching, or with the daily conflicts with the civilian academic authorities and the military hierarchy. Through his outbursts, he hastened the demise of the school. He had obeyed the King in forming military instructors by an accelerated method. But he had better things to do than to fabricate second lieutenants, a type that will never be lacking in any society. What is more, he solemnly warned his students that they should never try to militate for the establishment of universal teaching in the army. But neither should they forget that they had witnessed an *adventure* of the mind a little greater than the fabrication of subaltern officers:

> You formed subalterns in a few months, it's true.
> But to persist in obtaining results as paltry as those of the European schools, civil as much as military, is to spoil universal teaching.
> Let society profit from your experiences and be content with them, that will make me happy: you will be useful to the State.
> But never forget that you have seen results of a much superior order to those you have obtained and to which you will be reduced.
> Make use, then, of intellectual emancipation for the benefit of yourselves and your children. Help the poor.
> But for your country, confine yourselves to making subalterns and academic citizens.
> You no longer need me to move forward in that rut. [3]

This speech by the Founder to his military disciples—he had some faithful ones—appears on the frontispiece of the *Mathematics* volume of *Universal Teaching*, a work in which, in keeping with the master's frustrating habit in every matter, there isn't a single word about mathematics. No one is a disciple of universal teaching if he hasn't read that work as the history of the Ecole

Normale in Louvain; if he isn't convinced of this opinion: universal teaching isn't and cannot be a *social* method. It cannot be propagated in and by social institutions. The *emancipated* are undoubtedly respectful of the social order. They know that it is, in any case, less bad than disorder. But that's all that they grant it, and no institution can be satisfied with this minimum. It's not enough for inequality to be respected; it wants to be believed and loved. It wants to be *explicated*. Every institution is an *explication* in social act, a dramatization of inequality. Its principle is and always will be antithetical to that of a method based on equality and the refusal of explications. Universal teaching can only be directed to individuals, never to societies.

Human societies, united in nations, from the Laplanders to the Patagonians, need form for their stability, some kind of order. Those who are responsible for maintaining the necessary order must explain and have it explained that this order is the best of all orders, and they must prevent any contradictory explanation. This is the goal of constitutions and laws. Every social order, relying on an explication, thus excludes all other explications and especially rejects the method of intellectual emancipation, based as it is on the futility and even the danger of explication in teaching. The Founder even went so far as to recognize that the citizen of a state must respect the social order he's a part of, as well as the explication of that order; but he also established that the law only asked of a citizen that he conform his actions and words to this order, and could not impose thoughts, opinions, or beliefs on him; that the inhabitant of a country, before being a citizen, was a man; that the family was a sanctuary where the father was the supreme arbiter, and that consequently, it was there and there alone that intellectual emancipation could be fruitfully sown.[4]

Let's affirm, then, that universal teaching *will not take*, it will not be established in society. But *it will not perish*, because it is the natural method of the human mind, that of all people who look for their path themselves. What the disciples can do is to announce to all individuals, to all mothers and fathers, the way to teach what one doesn't know on the principle of the equality of intelligence.

Emancipation of Men and Instruction of the People

It must be announced to *everyone*. First, undoubtedly, to the poor: they have no other way to educate themselves if they can't pay the salaried explicators or spend long years on school benches. And above all, it is on them that the prejudice of the inequality of intelligence weighs most heavily. It is they who must be raised up from their humiliated position. Universal teaching is the poor's method.

But it isn't a method *of* the poor. It's a method of men, that is to say, of inventors. Whoever employs it, no matter what his science or his rank, will multiply his intellectual powers. It must therefore be announced to princes, ministers, and the powerful: they cannot *institute* universal teaching, but they can apply it to teach their children. And they can make use of their social prestige to announce the service far and wide. Thus the enlightened King of the Netherlands would have done better to teach his children what he didn't know, and to speak out for the diffusion of emancipatory ideas to families throughout the kingdom. Thus Joseph Jacotot's former colleague, General Lafayette, could announce it to the President of the United States, a new country not weighed down by centuries of scholastic stultification. In the days following the July Revolution of 1830, the Founder left Louvain for Paris to indicate to the victorious liberals and progressives the means of realizing their good thoughts regarding the people: General Lafayette had only to spread universal teaching throughout the national guard. Casimir Périer, former enthusiast of the doctrine and future Prime Minister, was now in a position to spread the service far and wide. Barthe, Laffitte's Minister of Public Instruction, came himself to consult with Joseph Jacotot: what must he do to organize the education that the government owes the people and that he intends to give them according to the best methods? Nothing, answered the Founder; government doesn't owe the people an education, for the simple reason that one doesn't owe people what they can take for themselves. And education is like liberty: it isn't given; it's taken. So what must be done? asked the minister. You need only announce, he replied, that I am in Paris at the Corneille Hotel, where every day I receive fathers of poor families to show them the means of emancipating their children.

It must be told to all those who worry about science or the people, or both. The learned should also learn it: they have the means of increasing their intellectual power tenfold. They think they are only capable of teaching what they know. We are aware of that social logic of false modesty where what one renounces establishes the solidity of what one announces. But scholars— those who research, certainly, not those who explicate the knowledge of others—perhaps want something a little newer and a little less conventional. Let them begin teaching what they don't know, and maybe they will discover unsuspected intellectual powers that will put them on the road to new discoveries.

It must be told to republicans who want a free and equal people and who imagine that this is a matter of laws and constitutions. It must be told to all men of progress, who, with generous hearts and fiery brains—inventors, philanthropists, and lovers of mathematics, polytechnicians and philotechnicians, Fourierists and Saint-Simonians—scour the countries of Europe and the fields of knowledge in search of technical inventions, agronomical ameliorations, economic formulas, pedagogical methods, moral institutions, architectural revolutions, typographical procedures, encyclopedic publications, etc., for the physical, intellectual, and moral improvement of the poorest and most numerous class. They can do much more for the poor than they think, and at less expense. They spend time and money experimenting with and promoting grainlofts and middens, fertilizer and conservation methods, in an attempt to improve cultivation and enrich the peasants, to clean the rot out of farm streams and the prejudices out of rustic minds. It is much simpler than that: with a used copy of *Télémaque*, or even a pen and some paper to write down a prayer, they can emancipate the inhabitants of the countryside, make them conscious of their intellectual power; and the peasants themselves will set about improving cultivation and grain conservation. *Stultification* is not an inveterate superstition; it is fear in the face of liberty. Routine is not ignorance; it is the cowardice and pride of people who renounce their own power for the unique pleasure of affirming their neighbor's incapacity. It is enough to *emancipate*. Don't ruin yourselves by inundating lawyers, notaries, and pharmacists of subprefectures with encyclopedic volumes intended to teach the inhabitants of the countryside the healthiest ways to preserve eggs, brand sheep, hasten melon ripening, salt butter, disinfect water, fabricate beet sugar, and make beer out of pea pods. Show them rather how to make their son repeat "Calypso," "Calypso could," "Calypso could not," and you will see what they can do.

Such is the unique chance, the unique chance of intellectual emancipation: each citizen is also a man who makes a *work*, with the pen, with the drill, or with any other tool. Each superior inferior is also an equal who recounts and is in turn told by another, the story of what he has seen. It is always possible to play with this relation of self to self, to bring it back to its primary veracity and waken the reasonable man in social man. Whoever doesn't seek to introduce the method of universal teaching into the workings of the social machine may awaken that entirely new energy that fascinated lovers of liberty, that power without gravity or agglomeration that is propagated in a flash by the contact between two poles. Whoever forsakes the workings of the social machine has the opportunity to make the electrical energy of emancipation circulate.

Only the stultified followers of the Old Master and those powerful in the old mode will be cast aside. They were already anxious about the evils of instruction for the sons of the people, imprudently cut off from their condition. What is speaking about emancipation and the equality of intelligence worth, if it is only to say that husband and wife have the same intelligence! A visitor had already asked Jacotot if women in these circumstances would still be pretty! Let's deprive the stultified of a response, then, and let them turn about within their academico-noble circle. We know that it is this that defines the stultifying vision of the world: to believe in the reality of inequality, to imagine that the superiors in society are truly superior, and that society would be in danger if the idea should spread, especially among the lower classes, that this superiority is only a conventional fiction. In fact, only an emancipated person is untroubled by the idea that the social order is entirely conventional; only he can scrupulously obey superiors that he knows are his equals. He knows what he can expect of the social order and will not make a big to-do about it. The stultified have nothing to fear, but they will never know it.

Men of Progress

Let's leave them, then, to the sweet and anxious consciousness of their genius. But standing right beside them is no lack of men of progress who shouldn't fear the overturning of the old intellectual hierarchies. We understand men of *progress* in the literal sense of the term: men who *move forward*, who are not concerned with the social rank of someone who has affirmed such and such a thing, but go see for themselves if the thing is true; voyagers who traverse Europe in search of all the procedures, methods, or institutions worthy of being imitated; who, when they have heard tell of some new experiment here or there, go to see the facts, try to reproduce the experiment; who don't see why six years should be spent learning something, if it's been proved that it can be done in two; who think, above all, that knowledge is nothing in itself and that *doing* is everything, that the sciences are pursued not to be explicated but to produce new discoveries and useful inventions; who therefore, when they hear about profitable inventions, are not content to praise them or critique them, but instead offer, if possible, their factory or their land, their capital or their devotion, to give them a *try*.

There is no lack of voyagers and innovators of this kind who are interested in, even enthusiastic, about possible applications of the Jacotot method. They might be teachers in conflict with the Old Master like Professor Durietz, nourished since his youth on Locke and Condillac, Helvetius and Condorcet, who had early on mounted an assault on "the dusty edifice of our Gothic institutions."[5] A professor at the central school in Lille, he had founded in that city an establishment inspired by the principles of his masters. A victim of the Emperor's "consuming hatred" for the ideologues, for "any institution that didn't go along with his goal of universal servitude," but still devoted to shaking off *backward* methods, he went to the Netherlands to undertake the education of the son of the Prussian ambassador, the Prince of Hatzfeldt. It is there that he heard about the Jacotot method, visited the establishment that a former polytechnician, de Séprès, had founded on those principles, recognized their conformity with his own, and decided to propagate the method wherever he could. This is what he did for five years in Saint Petersburg at Grand Marshal Paschov's, at Prince Sherbretov's, and at the homes of several other dignitaries who were friends of progress, before returning to France—not without propagating emancipation en route, at Riga and Odessa, in Germany and Italy. He now wanted to "chop down the tree of abstractions" and, if he could, pull it out "by the fibers of its deepest roots."[6]

He spoke about his projects to Ternaux, the famous textile manufacturer and a deputy of the extreme liberal Left. No more enlightened industrialist could be found: Ferdinand Ternaux was not content to reorganize his father's tottering factory and make it prosper during the troubling times of the Revolution and the Empire. He wanted to be useful to the national industry in general, by favoring the production of cashmere. To this end, he recruited an orientalist from the Bibliothèque Nationale and sent him to Tibet to find a herd of fifteen hundred goats to be acclimatized to the Pyrenees. An ardent friend of liberty and the Enlightenment, he wanted to see for himself the results of the Jacotot method. Convinced, he promised his support, and with his help, Durietz felt strengthened in his quest to annihilate the "dealers in supines and gerunds" and other "satraps of the university monopoly."

Ferdinand Ternaux was not the only industrialist to move ahead in this way. In Mulhouse, the Industrial Society, an institution pioneered by the philanthropical dynamism of the Dollfus brothers, confided a course in universal teaching for workers to the care of its young animator, Doctor Penot. In Paris, a more modest industrialist, the dyer Beauvisage, heard tell of the method. A worker who had made it on his own, he wanted to extend his affairs by founding a new factory in the Somme. But in so doing, he didn't want to be separated from the workers, the brothers of his origins. A republican and freemason, he dreamed of making his workers his associates. Unfortunately, this dream ran up against an unpleasant reality. In his factory, as in all the others, the workers were envious of each other and only got along when in opposition to the master. He wanted to give them the education that would destroy the old man in them and would permit the realization of his ideal. For this, he addressed himself to the Ratier brothers, fervent disciples of the method, one of whom preached emancipation every Sunday in the Halle aux Draps.

In addition to the industrialists, there were progressive military men, ingenious officers principally of the artillery, guardians of the revolutionary and polytechnic tradition. Thus Lieutenant Schölcher, the son of a rich porcelain maker and an officer of genius at Valenciennes, went regularly to visit Joseph Jacotot, who had temporarily retired there. One day he brought with him his brother Victor, who wrote in various newspapers, who had visited the United States and returned indignant that there could still exist in the nineteenth century that denial of humanity called slavery.

But the archetype of all these progressives was surely the

Count of Lasteyrie, a septuagenarian and president, founder, or mainspring of the Society for the Encouragement of National Industry, the Society for Elementary Education, the Society for Mutual Teaching, the Central Society for Agronomy, the Philanthropic Society, the Society of Teaching Methods, the Vaccine Society, the Asian Society, the *Journal d'éducation et d'instruction*, and the *Journal des connaissances usuelles*. Please don't snicker, imagining some pot-bellied academician, peacefully snoozing away in presidential armchairs. On the contrary, de Lasteyrie was known for not staying in one place. In his youth, he had visited England, Italy, and Switzerland to perfect his knowledge of economics and improve the management of his domains. At first a partisan of the Revolution like his brother-in-law, the Marquis de Lafayette, he nevertheless, toward Year III, was obliged to go hide his title in Spain. There he learned the language well enough to translate various anticlerical works, studied merino sheep well enough to publish two books on the subject, and appreciated their merits well enough to bring a herd back to France. He traveled through Holland, Denmark, Sweden (whence he brought back rutabaga), Norway, and Germany. He looked into the fattening of livestock, into the appropriate kinds of pits for grain storage, into the cultivation of cotton, and of indigo plants and vegetables that produce the color blue. In 1812 he learned of Alois Senefelder's invention of lithography. He immediately left for Munich, learned the process, and created the first lithographic press in France. The pedagogical power of this new industry oriented him toward questions of education. He was then militating for the introduction of mutual teaching using the Lancastrian method. But he wasn't at all exclusive. Among other societies, he founded the Society of Teaching Methods for the study of all pedagogical innovations. Alerted by public rumor of the miracles being produced in Belgium, he decided to go see them for himself.

Still alert at seventy years old—he would live twenty more, writing books and founding societies and journals to cleave obscurantism asunder and promote science and philosophy—he took the mail carriage, saw the Founder, visited Miss Marcellis's institution, gave improvisations and compositions to the students to do, and verified that they wrote as well as he did. The opinion of the equality of intelligence didn't frighten him. He saw in it a great encouragement to the acquisition of science and virtue, a blow far more deadly than any material power to be struck against the intellectual aristocracy. He hoped that its exactitude could be shown. So, he thought, "the pretensions of those proud geniuses would disappear, those who, believing themselves privileged by nature, believe themselves equally in the right to dominate their fellow-men and to reduce them to the level of beasts, so as to enjoy exclusively the material gifts that blind fortune distributes and that are known to be acquired by profiting from human ignorance."[7] He came back to announce it to the Society of Teaching Methods: an immense step had just been taken for civilization and the happiness of the human species. It was a new method that the society must examine and recommend to the first rank of those best suited to hasten the progress of the people's education.

Of Sheep and Men

Jacotot appreciated the count's zeal. But he was immediately obliged to denounce his *distraction*. It was strange, in fact, for someone who applauded the idea of intellectual emancipation to then submit it to the approbation of a Society of Methods. What exactly is a *Society of Methods*? An Areopagus of superior minds who want mass education and try to select the best methods of arriving at it. This evidently supposes that poor families are incapable of selecting on their own. For that they would have to be already educated. In such a case, they wouldn't need instruction. In such a case, there would be no need for the society—which is contradictory with the hypothesis.

It's a very old ruse, the learned society one, by which the world has always been duped and probably always will be. The public is fore-

stalled from taking the pains to examine things. The *Journal* is in
charge of seeing, the Society takes care of judging; and to give themselves an air of importance that intimidates the lazy, they don't praise,
never blame, neither too much nor too little. Only a small mind ad-
mires unreservedly; but by praising or blaming in a measured fashion,
besides gaining a reputation for impartiality, one is thus placed above
those one judges, one is worth more than they, one has wisely sorted
out the good from the mediocre and the bad. The report is an excellent
stultifying explication that cannot help being successful. Several little
axioms are invoked in addition, and used to interlard one's speech:
"Nothing is perfect," "One must mistrust exaggeration," "Time will
tell." . . . One of these characters takes the floor and says: My dear
friends, we agree among ourselves that all good methods will be put
to our test, and that the French nation will have confidence in the
results that derive from our analysis. The people out in the depart-
ments cannot have societies like ours to direct their judgments. Here
and there, in some of the big towns, there are some little testing
places; but the best test, the test par excellence, is only found in Paris.
All the good methods compete for the honor of being refined, verified
by our test. Only one purports to revolt; but, we insist, it will fade
like the others. The members' intelligence is the vast laboratory
wherein the legitimate analysis of all methods is performed. In vain
does Universal Teaching argue against our rules; they give us the right
to judge it, and we will judge it.[8]

Yet don't think that the Society of Methods judged the Jacotot method with ill-will. It shared its president's progressive
ideas and knew how to recognize *all that was good* in the method.
Undoubtedly a few snickering voices were raised in the Areopagus of professors to denounce this marvelous simplification
brought to the job of teaching. Undoubtedly some minds remained skeptical when confronted with the "curious details"
that their "indefatigable president" brought back from his voyage. Other voices besides made themselves heard denouncing
the charlatan's dramatization, the carefully prepared visits, the
"improvisations" learned by heart, the "original" compositions
copied from the master's books, books that opened all by themselves to the same spot. They also laughed about the master who

didn't know how to play guitar whose student played a different melody from the one he had under his eyes.[9] But the members of the Society of Methods weren't men to believe one report. Froussard, a skeptic, went to verify de Lasteyrie's report and came back convinced. Boutmy verified Froussard's enthusiasm, then Baudoin Boutmy's. All returned convinced. But they all returned equally convinced precisely of the eminent *progress* that this new teaching method represented. They weren't at all concerned with announcing it to the poor, with using it to instruct their children, or with using it to teach what they didn't know. They asked that the society adopt it for the *"orthomatic"* school it was organizing, something that would demonstrate the excellence of the new methods. The majority of the society and de Lasteyrie himself opposed this: the society could not adopt one method "to the exclusion of all those that present themselves or that will present themselves later on." That would "prescribe limits to perfectibility" and destroy the central tenet of the society's philosophical faith and its practical reason for being: the progressive perfecting of *all* good methods—past, present, and future.[10] The society refused the *exaggeration*, but, imperturbably serene and objective in the face of the jeers about universal teaching, it allocated a room in the orthomatic school to the Jacotot method of teaching.

Such was de Lasteyrie's inconsistency: in earlier days he hadn't thought to convoke a commission on the value of merino sheep or lithography, to make a report on the necessity of importing one or the other. He imported them himself so he could try them out on his own. But he judged differently when it came to importing emancipation: this was for him a public affair that must be treated by society. This unfortunate difference was itself based on an unfortunate identification; he confused people to be educated with a flock of sheep. Flocks of sheep don't drive themselves, and he thought it was the same for men: certainly they had to be emancipated, but it was up to enlightened minds to do it, and for that, all ideas should be put in common in order to find the best methods, the best instruments of emancipation.

Emancipation for him meant putting light in obscurity's place, and he thought that the Jacotot method was one method of instruction like the others, a system for enlightening minds comparable to the others: an invention that was certainly excellent but of the same nature as all those that proposed, week after week, a new perfecting of the perfecting of the people's education: Bricaille's panlexigraphy, Dupont's citology, Montemont's stiquiotechnics, Ottin's stereometrics, Painpare and Lupin's typography, Coulon-Thevenot's tachygraphy, Fayet's stenography, Carstairs's calligraphy, Jazwinski's Polish method, the Gallic method, the Lévi method, the methods of Senocq, Coupe, Lacombe, Mesnager, Schlott, Alexis de Noailles, and a hundred others whose books and memoirs piled up on the society's desk. From then on, everything was set: society, commission, examination, report, journal, *there's good and bad in it*, *time will tell*, *nec probatis nec improbatis*, and so on until the end of time.

When it was a question of agricultural and industrial improvements, de Lasteyrie had acted in the manner of universal teaching: he had seen, compared, reflected, imitated, tried, corrected by himself. But when it was a matter of announcing intellectual emancipation to the fathers of poor and ignorant families, he was *distracted*, he forgot everything. He translated equality as PROGRESS and the emancipation of the fathers of poor families as EDUCATING THE PEOPLE. And in order to be concerned with these abstractions, these *ontologies*, other abstractions—corporations—were necessary. A man can drive a herd of sheep. But for the herd PEOPLE, a herd called LEARNED SOCIETY, UNIVERSITY, COMMISSION, REVIEW, etc., was necessary—in short, stultification, the old rule of the social fiction. Intellectual emancipation pretended to replace it. Yet it found stultification there on its own route, erected as a tribunal charged with trying out universal teaching's principles and exercises for their suitability or unsuitability to families, and with judging it in the name of progress, and indeed in the name of the emancipation of the people.

The Progressives' Circle

The inconsistency did not owe simply to de Lasteyrie's weary brain. It was the contradiction that intellectual emancipation meets head on when it addresses itself to those—the men of progress—who want, just as it does, the happiness of the poor. The oracle of stultification had warned the Founder well: "Today more than ever, you cannot hope for success. They believe themselves to be progressing, and their opinions are solidly hinged on this. I laugh at your efforts; they will not budge."

The contradiction is easy to expose. We said: a man of progress is a man who moves forward, who goes to see, experiments, changes his practice, verifies his knowledge, and so on without end. This is the literal definition of the word progress. But now a man of progress is something else as well: a man whose thinking takes the *opinion* of progress as its point of departure, who erects that opinion to the level of the dominant explication of the social order.

We know, in fact, that explication is not only the stultifying weapon of pedagogues but the very bond of the social order. Whoever says order says distribution into ranks. Putting into ranks presupposes explication, the distributory, justificatory fiction of an inequality that has no other reason for being. The day-to-day work of explication is only the small change of the dominant explication that characterizes a society. Wars and revolutions change the nature of dominant explications by changing the form and limits of empires. But this change is narrowly circumscribed. We know, in fact, that explication is the work of laziness. It need only introduce inequality, and that is done at little expense. The most elementary hierarchy is that of *good* and *evil*. The simplest logical relationship that can serve to explain this hierarchy is that of *before* and *after*. With these four terms, good and evil, before and after, we have the matrix of all explications. Things were better before, say some: the legislator or the divinity arranged things; people were frugal and happy, leaders paternal and obeyed, the ancestors' faith respected, functions well distributed, and hearts united. Now, words are corrupted, distinctions crumble, ranks are confused, and solicitude for the young has been lost, along with respect for the aged. Let's try then to preserve or revive that which, in our distinctions, still holds us to the principle of the good. Happiness will come tomorrow, respond the others: the human species was like a child left to the caprices and terrors of his imagination, rocked to sleep with ignorant nursemaids' fairytales, subjected to the brutal force of despots and priestly superstition. Now, minds are enlightened, customs are civilized, and industry spreads its benefits; people know their rights, and education will reveal to them their duties with science. *Capacity* must from now on decide social ranks. And it is education that will reveal and develop it.

We are at the moment when a dominant explication is in the process of succumbing to another's conquering force: an age of transition. And this is what explains the inconsistency of men of progress like the count. Before, when the university blundered through *Barbara*, *Celarent*, and *Baralipton*, there were, *outside of it*, gentlemen or doctors, bourgeois or Church people, who allowed it to go on speaking and were busy doing something else: they had lenses cut and polished, or polished them themselves for optical experiments; they had their butchers save them animals' eyes so they could study anatomy; they informed each other of their discoveries and debated each other's hypotheses. Thus, in the pores of the old society, *progress*—that is, realizations of the human capacity to understand and to do— was accomplished. The count still resembles these experimental gentlemen a little. But as time passed, he had been snatched up by the rising force of the new explication, the new inequality: Progress. It is no longer the curious and the fault-finders who perfect one or another branch of the sciences, such and such a technical method. It's *society* that perfects *itself*, that takes perfectibility as the watchword of its order. It's society that progresses, and a society can only progress socially, that is to say, all together and in good order. Progress is the new way of saying inequality.

But that way of saying it has a much more formidable force than the old way. The latter was continually obliged to go against the grain of its principle. Things were better before, it said; the more we advance, the closer we get to decadence. But this dominant opinion had the shortcoming of not being applicable to the dominant explicatory practice—that of pedagogues. These people were certainly obliged to suppose that the child approached his perfection by being distanced from his origin, by growing up and progressing under their direction from his ignorance to their science. Every pedagogical practice explains the inequality of knowledge as an evil, and a reducible evil in an indefinite progression toward the good. All pedagogy is spontaneously progressive. Thus there was a discordance between the grand explication and the little explicators. Both were stultifying, but in a disorderly fashion. And this disorder within stultification left some space open for emancipation.

Those times were ending. Thereafter, the dominant fiction and the daily stultification went in the same direction. There is a simple reason for this. Progress is the pedagogical fiction built into the fiction of the society as a whole. At the heart of the pedagogical fiction is the representation of inequality as a *retard* in one's development: inferiority, in its innocence, lets itself be taken in; neither a lie nor violence, inferiority is only a lateness, a delay, that is posited so one can put oneself in the position of curing it. Of course, this will never happen: nature itself makes sure of it; there will always be delay, always inequality. But one can thus continually exercise the privilege of reducing it, and there are double benefits to be gained from this.

The progressives' presuppositions are the social absolutizing of what is presupposed by pedagogy: before, steps were taken gropingly, blindly; words were gathered more or less badly from the mouths of unenlightened mothers or nursemaids; things were guessed at, false ideas drawn from the first contact with the material universe. Now, a new age is beginning, the one where the man-child takes the right road to maturity. The guide points to the veil covering all things and begins to raise it— suitably, in order, step by step, *progressively*. "A certain delay must be worked into the progress."[11] Methods are necessary. Without a method, without a *good* method, the child-man or the people-child is prey to childish fictions, to routine and prejudices. With a method, he sets his feet in the footsteps of those who advance rationally, progressively. He grows up in their wake in an indefinite process of coming closer. Never will the student catch up with the master, nor the people with its enlightened elite; but the hope of getting there makes them advance along the good road, the one of perfected explications. The century of Progress is that of the triumphant explicators, of humanity pedagogicized. The formidable force of this new stultification is that it still imitates the approach of the men of progress of a former day; it attacks the old stultification in terms that will put minds just alerted to emancipation on the wrong scent, will make them stumble at the slightest distraction.

This is also to say that the ongoing victory of the progressives over the Old Master is just as much the Old Master's victory by virtue of their very opposition: the absolute triumph of institutionalized inequality, the exemplary rationalization of that institution. And this is the solid foundation on which the perennial power of the Old Master is based. The Founder tried to show this to the progressives of good faith: "The explicators of industry and everyone have already repeated: look at civilization's progress! The people need arts, and we sold them only Latin they can't use. They will draw, design machines, etc. Philosophers, you are right, and I admire your zeal under the reign of a Great Master who doesn't help you at all, lounging lazily on his throne of dead languages. I admire your devotion; your philanthropical goal is undoubtedly more useful than that of the Old Master. But aren't your ways the same as his? Isn't your method the same? Aren't you afraid of being accused of sustaining, as he does, the supremacy of the master explicators?"[12]

Goodwill thus risks becoming an aggravating circumstance. The Old Master knows what he wants—stultification—and he works to that end. The progressives, on the other hand, want to liberate minds and promote the abilities of the masses. But what they propose is to perfect stultification by perfecting explications.

This is the progressives' circle. They want to tear minds away from the old routine, from the control of priests and obscurantists of any kind. And for that, more rational explications and methods are necessary. They must be tested and compared by way of commissions and reports. A qualified and licensed personnel, learned in the new methods and monitored on their execution of them, must be employed to educate the people. Above all, the improvisations of incompetents must be avoided; one must not permit minds formed by chance or routine, ignorant of the perfected explications and progressive methods, to have the possibility of opening a school and teaching anything in any which way. Families—those places of the routine reproducing of inveterate superstition, of empirical knowledge and obscure sentiment—must be prevented from taking on their children's instruction. For this, a well-ordered system of public instruction is necessary. A University and a Great Master are necessary. It will be pointed out in vain that the Greeks and Romans had neither a University nor a Great Master, and that things didn't go badly for them. In the era of progress, the most ignorant of backward peoples need no more than a brief stay in Paris to be convinced that "Anytus and Meletus demonstrated from that point on the necessity of an organization that determines (1) that one must explicate; (2) what one will explicate; (3) how one will explicate it." Without these precautions, they see clearly that "(1) our shoemakers might put *universal teaching* around the boot on their signs, as was done in Rome or Athens, for want of a careful organization, [and] (2) the tailor will want to explain developable surfaces, without any previous examination, as occurred in Rome," with the result that what must at all costs be avoided will come to pass: "the old explications will be transmitted from age to age to the detriment of perfected explications."[13]

The perfecting of instruction is thus first the perfecting of *tethers*, or rather the perfecting of the representation of the usefulness of tethers. The permanent pedagogical revolution becomes the normal regime under which the explicatory institution is rationalized and justified, assuring at the same time the perpetuity of the old method's principles and institutions. By fighting for the new methods, for Lancaster's mutual teaching, the progressives fought first to show the necessity of having better tethers. "You know that we don't want Lancaster at all, and you have figured out why. And yet we've ended up letting you do your Lancaster. Do you know why? It's that the tether is still there. It will be better held by different hands. But one need never despair wherever there is a tether. Your applied geometry doesn't appeal to *us* either, but it can nevertheless be formally applied."[14] They let the Lancastrian method get by; soon, undoubtedly, they'll let industrial teaching get by. It was a tether, as good as any other tether, less for what it could furnish in the way of instruction than for what it could *make people believe* about the inegalitarian fiction. It was another riding-school that would oppose the old one only to better affirm its principle, the principle of all riding-schools. "They were circling around in Latin; the riding master will make them circle around in machines. . . . If we don't watch out, stultification is going to become greater because less noticeable and easier to justify."[15]

On the Heads of the People

Let's go farther. Universal teaching can also become a "good method" integrated into this renovation of stultification: a *natural* method that respects the intellectual development of the child all the while procuring for his mind the best of gymnastics; an *active* method that makes him habituated to reasoning for himself and confronting difficulties alone, that creates self-assurance in speech and a sense of responsibility; a good *classical* foundation, learning language at the school of the great writers, disdaining grammarians' jargon; a practical and *expeditious* method that does away with the costly and interminable stages of college to form enlightened and industrious young people, ready to launch themselves into careers useful for the perfecting of society. Whoever can do the most can do the least, and a method used to teach what one doesn't know permits teaching by playing with what one knows. Good masters are opening schools under its name, proven masters like Durietz; like the young Eugène Boutmy; like de Séprès, the former polytechnician, who moved his institution from Anvers to Paris; and a swarm of others, in Paris, Rouen, Metz, Clermont-Ferrand, Poitiers, Lyon, Grenoble, Nantes, Marseille. Not to mention religious and more or less enlightened institutions, like the Institute of the Word Incarnate, where Guillard, who had made the trip to Louvain, gives courses based on "Know yourself," like those seminars in Pamiers, Senlis, and elsewhere, converted by the indefatigable zeal of the disciple Deshoullières. These institutions—we do not speak, to be sure, of the counterfeits that proliferated—are commendable in the exactitude with which they follow the method's exercises: "Calypso," "Calypso could," "Calypso could not"; and, after that, the improvisations, compositions, verifications, synonyms, etc. In short, all of Jacotot's teaching is respected there except in one or two small matters: they are not teaching what they don't know. But not everyone who wants to be can be ignorant, and it isn't Boutmy's fault if he trained in ancient languages, or de Séprès's, if he is a mathematician, and one of the best at that.

The prospectuses don't talk about the equality of intelligence either. But this, as we know, is an *opinion* of the Founder. And he himself taught us to separate opinions strictly from facts and to base any demonstration only on the latter. What good is it to startle skeptical or half-convinced minds with the brutal preliminary of that opinion? It's better to put facts in front of them, the results of the method, to show them the principle's strength. This is also why Jacotot's name is not broadcasted and dishonored. Instead they speak of the *natural method*, a method recognized by the best minds of the past: Socrates and Montaigne, Locke and Condillac. Hadn't the master himself said that there was no Jacotot method, only the student's method, the natural method of the human mind? So what good would it do to brandish his name like a fan? As early as 1828, Durietz had warned the Founder that he wanted to chop down "the tree of abstractions," but he wouldn't do it like a woodcutter. He wanted to creep slowly and engineer "several ostensible successes" in order to prepare the method's triumph. He wanted to move toward intellectual emancipation through universal teaching.[16]

But the victorious revolution of 1830 offered a more grandiose theater for that effort. The occasion arose in 1831, provided by the most modern of the progressives, the young journalist Emile de Girardin. He was twenty-six years old. He was the grandson of the Marquis de Girardin who had protected *Emile*'s author. It's true he was a bastard, but this was the start of a new era when no one had to blush about one's birth. He was one with the new era and the new forces: work and industry; professional instruction and domestic economy; public opinion and the press. He laughed at Latinists and pedants. He laughed at the young fools the good provincial families sent to Paris to study law and flirt with working-girls. He wanted active elites, lands fertilized by the latest chemical discoveries, a people educated in everything that could lead to its material happiness, and enlightened on the balance of rights, duties, and interests that creates the equilibrium of modern societies. He wanted all this to come about very fast, for youth to be prepared by rapid methods to become useful to the community at an early age, for the discoveries of scholars and inventors to become part of the life of workshops and households immediately, even in the most distant countryside, so new thoughts might be engendered. He wanted an organ to disseminate these benefits without delay. Of course, there was de Lasteyrie's *Journal des connaissances usuelles*. But this kind of publication was expensive and thus inevitably reserved for a public who had no need of it. What good was it to vulgarize science for academics and domestic science for women of high society? So he launched the *Journal des connaissances utiles* in an edition of a hundred thousand copies through a gigantic subscription and advertising campaign. To sustain the journal and prolong its action, he founded a new society and called it simply the National Society for Intellectual Emancipation.

The principle of that emancipation was simple. "For constitutions as for edifices, a firm and level soil is necessary. Instruction gives intelligence a level, a soil for ideas. . . . Instruction for the masses puts absolutist governments in danger. Their ignorance, on the other hand, is perilous to republican governments, for though the masses can learn of their rights through parliamentary debates, they cannot be expected to exercise them with discernment. As soon as a people knows its rights, there is only one way to govern it, and that is to instruct it. Thus, what is necessary to every republican government is a vast system of graduated teaching, national and professional, that sheds light onto the dark souls of the masses, that replaces all arbitrary demarcations, that assigns each class to its rank, each man to his place."[17]

This new order was, of course, that of the recognized dignity of the laboring population, of its preponderant place in the social order. Intellectual emancipation was the overturning of the old hierarchy attached to instruction's privilege. Until that time, instruction had been the monopoly of the managing classes justifying their hegemony, with the well-known consequence that an educated child of the people no longer wanted his parents' life. The social logic of the system had to be overturned. From now on instruction would no longer be a privilege; rather, the lack of instruction would be an *incapacity*. To oblige the people to get educated, any man of twenty who could not read in 1840 should be declared an incapable civilian. One of the first numbers from the drawing that condemned unlucky young people to military service must be officially reserved for him. This obligation contracted with the people was just as

much an obligation contracted against it. Expeditious methods
to teach all French youth how to read before 1840 had to be
found. This would be the National Society for Intellectual
Emancipation's motto: "Pour instruction onto the heads of the
people; you owe it this baptism."

Over the baptismal font stood the secretary of the society, the
rake from the Society of Methods, universal teaching's enthusiastic admirer, Eugène Boutmy. In the journal's first issue, he
promised to indicate expeditious methods for educating the
masses. He kept his word in an article entitled "Teaching by
Oneself." The master should read aloud "Calypso" and the student repeat "Calypso"; then, separating the words well, "Calypso could," "Calypso could not," etc. The method was called
natural universal teaching, in honor of nature itself, which taught
it to children. An honorable deputy, Victor de Tracy, had instructed forty peasants from his commune in this way with
enough success that they were able to write a letter in which
they poured out to him their deep gratitude for his having thus
ushered them into intellectual life. Let each reader of the *Journal* do the same, and soon the leprosy of ignorance would disappear entirely from the social body.[18]

The society, which wished to encourage exemplary institutions, was also interested in de Séprès's establishment. It sent
commissaries to examine that method of *"autodidaxy"* that
taught young boys to reflect, to speak and to reason from facts,
by following the natural method that had always been the vehicle of great discoveries. The establishment's location on the
rue de Monceau, in the Parisian quarter most known for its air,
the wholesomeness of its food, its hygiene, and its gymnastics,
as well as its moral and religious sentiments, left little to be
desired. And, in three years of secondary teaching, at a maxi-
mum price of eight hundred francs a year, the institution un-
dertook to bring its students to the point where they could pass
any examination. Thus, a father could foresee exactly how much
his son's education would cost and calculate whether it was
worthwhile. The society conferred on de Séprès's institution the

title National Lycée. On the other hand, it urged the parents who sent their children there to read the programs carefully so as to determine what career their sons should follow. That career determined, the society's commissaries watched to make sure that the course of study the parents wanted was scrupulously followed, so that the student would learn everything needed for a distinguished profession, and, above all, that he didn't learn *anything superfluous.*[19] Unfortunately, the commissaries hardly had time to pursue their collaboration with the National Lycée's work. A Breton agricultural institution, designed to spread agronomical knowledge at the same time that it regenerated part of the unemployed city youth, was the financial abyss into which the National Society for Intellectual Emancipation collapsed. At least it had sown seeds for the future: "It was a good journal, that useful knowledge one. We took your word about intellectual emancipation, and we are emancipating our subscribers by dint of explications. That kind of emancipation is not at all dangerous. When a horse is bridled and mounted by a good horseman, we know where we're going. He doesn't know anything, but we can be calm; he will not stray in the mountains and valleys."[20]

The Triumph of the Old Master

And so universal teaching and even the words intellectual emancipation could be put in the service of progressives who in fact worked to the Old Master's greatest profit. The division of labor worked this way: for the progressives, the methods and licenses, the reviews and journals maintaining the love of explications by the indefinite perfecting of their perfecting; for the Old Master, the institutions and the examinations, the administration of the solid foundations of the explicative institution, and the power of social sanction.

From there all those licensed inventions that collide with each other in the void of the explicatory system: explications of reading, writing metamorphosed, languages made simple, synoptical tables, perfected methods, etc., and so many other beautiful things, copied into new books containing a new explication of the old ones; everything recommended by the perfected explicators of our era, who all rightly make fun of each other as forerunners. Never have certified officers been more to be pitied than in our time. There are so many of them that they can hardly find a schoolchild who doesn't have his little perfected explication; to the point that they will soon be reduced to explicating to each other their respective explications. . . . The Old Master laughs at these disputes, excites them, names commissions to judge them; and, since the commissions approve all the perfectings, he doesn't part with his old scepter for anyone. *Divide and conquer.* The Old Master retains for himself the colleges, universities, and conservatories; he gives the others only what's left and tells them that's already a lot, and they believe it.

Like time, the explicatory system is nourished by its own children whom it devours as it produces them; a new explication, a new perfecting is born and immediately dies to make room for a thousand others. . . .

And thus the explicatory system is renewed, thus the Latin colleges and the Greek universities are maintained. People will cry out, but the colleges will endure. People will make fun of them, but the most learned and the most enlightened will continue to greet each other, humorlessly, in their old ceremonial suits; the young industrial method will insult its grandmother's scientific affectations, and yet the industrialists will still use their rulers and their perfected compasses to build a throne where the old driveler can sit and rule over all the workshops. In a word, the industrialists will make explicatory professorial chairs for as long as there is wood on the earth.[21]

Thus the victory in progress of the *luminous* over the *obscurantists* worked to rejuvenate the oldest cause defended by the obscurantists: the inequality of intelligence. There wasn't, in fact, any inconsistency in this division of roles. What the progressives' *distraction* was based on is the passion that underlies all distraction, the opinion of inequality. A progressive explicator is first of all an explicator, that is to say, a defender of inequality. It's very true that the social order doesn't require anyone to believe in inequality, nor does it prevent anyone from announcing emancipation to individuals and families. But that simple announcement—which there are never enough police to prevent—is also the one that meets the most impenetrable resistance: that of the intellectual hierarchy that has no other power except the rationalization of inequality. Progressivism is the modern form of that power, purified of any mixture with the material forms of traditional authority: progressives have *no power other* than that ignorance, that incapacity of the people on which their priesthood is based. How, without opening up an abyss under their own feet, can they say to working people that they don't need them in order to be free men, in order to be educated in everything suitable to their dignity as men? "Each one of these so-called emancipators has his herd of emancipated people whom he saddles, bridles, and spurs onward."[22] Thus, they all found themselves united in rejecting the only *bad* method, the *disastrous* method, that is to say, the method of *bad* emancipation, Jacotot's method—or rather, his anti-method.

Those who erased this proper name knew what they were doing. For it was the proper name that made all the difference, that said *equality of intelligence* and would have opened up the abyss underneath the feet of all the givers of instruction and of happiness to the people. The name need only be silenced for the *announcement* not to take place.

You cry out in vain in writing; those who don't know how to read can only learn from us what you have printed, and we would be very foolish to announce to them that they don't need our explications. If we give reading lessons to some, we will continue to use all the *good* methods, never those that could give the idea of intellectual emancipation. Let's make sure not to begin with having them read prayers; the child who knows them might think that he could have figured them out by himself. He must above all never know that he who knows how to read prayers can learn to read everything else by himself. . . . Let's make sure never to pronounce those emancipatory words: learning *and* relating.[23]

What had to be prevented above all was letting the poor know that they could educate themselves by their own abilities, that they had *abilities*—those abilities that in the social and political order now succeeded the old titles of nobility. And the best way to do this was to educate them, that is to say, to give them the measure of their inability. Schools were opened everywhere, and nowhere did anyone want to announce the possibility of learning without a master explicator. Intellectual emancipation had founded its "politics" on a principle: not to seek to penetrate social institutions, to work instead with individuals and families. But this was a moment when that separation, which was emancipation's only chance, was breaking down. Social institutions, intellectual corporations, and political parties now came knocking on families' doors, addressing themselves to all individuals for the purpose of educating them. Heretofore, the University and its baccalaureate had only controlled access to a few professions: a few thousand lawyers, doctors, and academics. All the other social careers were open to those who formed themselves in their own way. It wasn't, for example, necessary to have a baccalaureate to be a polytechnician. But with the system of perfected explications came the installation of the system of *perfected* examinations. From this point on, the Old Master, with the help of the perfecters, would increasingly use his examinations to curb the liberty to learn by any means other than his explications and the noble ascension of his degrees. The perfected examination, the exemplary representation of the master's omniscience and of the student's inability to ever equal him, was from that point on erected as the unbendable power of the inequality of intelligence over the path of whoever might wish to move through society at his own pace. Intellectual emancipation thus saw its retrenchments, the pockets of the old order, inexorably invested by the advances of the explicatory machine.

Society Pedagogicized

Everyone conspired in this, and especially those most passionately bent on the republic and the happiness of the people. Republicans take the sovereignty of the people as a principle,

but they *know very well* that the sovereign people cannot be identified with the ignorant swarm devoted solely to the defense of
its own material interests. They also *know very well* that the republic signifies the equality of rights and duties, but that it
cannot decree the equality of intelligence. It is clear, in fact,
that a backward peasant does not have the intelligence of a republican leader. Some think that this inevitable inequality derives from social diversity, like the infinite variety of leaves derives from the inexhaustible richness of nature. One need only
make sure that the inferior intelligence not be prevented from
understanding his rights and, especially, his duties. Others
think that time, little by little, progressively, will attenuate the
deficiency caused by centuries of oppression and obscurity. In
the two cases, equality's cause—good equality, nondisastrous
equality—has the same requisite, the instruction of the people:
the instruction of the ignorant by the learned, of men buried
in egotistical material concerns by men of devotion, of individuals enclosed in their particularities by the universality of reason
and public power. This is called public instruction, that is to
say, the instruction of the empirical people, programmed by the
representatives of the sovereign concept of the people.

Public Instruction is the secular arm of progress, the way to
equalize inequality progressively, that is to say, to unequalize
equality indefinitely. Everything is still played out according to
a sole principle, the inequality of intelligence. If this principle
is granted, then one consequence alone can logically be deduced
from it: the intelligent caste's management of the stupid mul-
titude. Republicans and all sincere men of progress feel heavy-
hearted at this consequence. All their efforts are directed at
agreeing with the principle without accepting the consequence.
This is what the eloquent author of the *Book of the People*, Félicité
Robert de Lamennais, makes clear: "Without a doubt," he recognizes *honestly*, "men do not possess equal faculties."[24] But
must the man of the people, for all that, be condemned to passive obedience, be brought down to the level of an animal? It
cannot be this way: "The sublime attribute of intelligence, self-

sovereignty, distinguishes the man from the brute."[25] Undoubtedly the unequal distribution of this sublime attribute imperils the "City of God" that the preacher urged the people to build. But it remains possible if the people know how to "use wisely" its regained rights. The ways that the man of the people might not be *brought down*, the ways that he might *use wisely* his rights, the ways to make equality out of inequality—this is the education of the people, that is to say, the interminable making up for its belatedness.

Such is the logic that puts things in their place, that of the "reduction" of inequalities. Whoever has consented to the fiction of the inequality of intelligence, whoever has refused the unique equality that the social order can allow, can do nothing but run from fiction to fiction, and from ontology to corporation, to reconcile the sovereign people with the retarded people, the inequality of intelligence with the reciprocity of rights and duties. Public Instruction, the instituted social fiction of inequality as lateness, is the magician that will reconcile all these reasonable beings. It will do it by infinitely extending the field of its explications and the examinations that control them. By this account, the Old Master will always win, supported by a new industrial pulpit and the luminous faith of the progressives.

Against this there is nothing else to do but to tell those supposedly sincere men again and again to pay more attention: "Change the form, untie the tether, break, break every pact with the Old Master. Realize that he is not any stupider than you. Reflect on this and you will tell me *what you think about it*."[26] But how could they ever understand the consequence? How could they understand that the mission of the luminous is not to enlighten those who dwell in obscurity? What man of science and devotion would accept in this way to leave his light under a basket and the salt of the earth without savor? And how would the fragile young plants, the childlike minds of the people, how would they grow without the beneficial dew of explications? Who could understand that the way for them to rise up in the intellectual order is not to learn what they don't know from scholars but rather to teach it to other ignorant ones? A man might, with a great deal of difficulty, understand this reasoning, but no *learned* person will ever understand it. Even Joseph Jacotot himself would never have understood it without the chance event that had turned him into the ignorant schoolmaster. Only chance is strong enough to overturn the instituted and incarnated belief in inequality.

And yet a *nothing* would be all that's necessary. It would suffice for the friends of the people, for one short instant, to fix their attention on this point of departure, on this first principle summed up in a very simple and very old metaphysical axiom: the nature of the totality cannot be the same as that of its parts. Whatever rationality is given to society is taken from the individuals that make it up. And what is refused to the individuals, society can easily take for itself, but it can never give it back to them. This goes for reason as it goes for equality, which is reason's synonym. One must choose to attribute reason to real individuals or to their fictive unity. One must choose between making an unequal society out of equal men and making an equal society out of unequal men. Whoever has some taste for equality shouldn't hesitate: individuals are real beings, and society a fiction. It's for real beings that equality has value, not for a fiction.

One need only learn how to be equal men in an unequal society. This is what *being emancipated* means. But this very simple thing is the hardest to understand, especially since the new explication—progress—has inextricably confused equality with its opposite. The task to which the republican hearts and minds are devoted is to make an equal society out of unequal men, to *reduce* inequality indefinitely. But whoever takes this position has only one way of carrying it through to the end, and that is the integral pedagogicization of society—the general infantilization of the individuals that make it up. Later on this will be called continuing education, that is to say, the coextension of the explicatory institution with society. The society of the superior inferiors will be equal, it will have reduced its inequalities once it has been entirely transformed into a society of explicated explicators.

Joseph Jacotot's singularity, his *madness*, was to have sensed this: his was the moment when the young cause of emancipation, that of the equality of men, was being transformed into the cause of social progress. And social progress was first of all progress in the social order's ability to be recognized as a rational order. This belief could only develop to the detriment of the emancipatory efforts of reasonable individuals, at the price of stifling the human potential embraced in the idea of equality. An enormous machine was revving up to promote equality through instruction. This was equality represented, socialized, made unequal, good for being *perfected*—that is to say, deferred from commission to commission, from report to report, from reform to reform, until the end of time. Jacotot was alone in recognizing the effacement of equality under progress, of emancipation under instruction. Let's understand this well. Outspoken anti-progressives were a dime a dozen in that century, and the atmosphere today, one of a fatigued progress, leads us to praise their lucidity. This is perhaps to give them too much honor: they merely hated equality. They hated progress because, like the progressives, they confused it with equality. Jacotot was the only *egalitarian* to perceive the representation and institutionalization of progress as a renouncing of the moral and intellectual adventure of equality, public instruction as the griefwork of emancipation. A knowledge of this sort makes for a frightening solitude. Jacotot assumed that solitude. He refused all progressive and pedagogical translation of emancipatory equality. On this point he agreed with the disciples who hid his name under the label "natural method": no one in Europe was strong enough to bear that name, the name of the madman. The name Jacotot was the proper name of that at once desperate and laughable knowledge of the equality of reasonable beings buried under the fiction of progress.

The Panecastic's Stories

There was nothing else to do but to maintain the gap attached to the proper name. Jacotot thus brought things into focus. For the progressives that came to see him, he had a *sieve* to put them through. When they became impassioned for the cause of equality in his presence, he softly said: "one can teach what one doesn't know." Unfortunately, the sieve worked too well. It was like trying to put a finger in the dike. The saying, they said unanimously, was *poorly chosen*. A little army of disciples tried to hold the flag against the professors of "natural" universal teaching. With them he proceeded in his way, tranquilly; he divided them into two groups: *teacher* or *explicator* disciples of the Jacotot method who sought to lead the students of universal teaching to intellectual emancipation; *emancipatory* disciples who taught only with emancipation as a preliminary, or who even taught nothing at all and were content to emancipate fathers by showing them how to teach their children what they didn't know. It goes without saying that he didn't hold the two in equal esteem: he preferred "an ignorant emancipated person, one alone, to a hundred million scholars taught by universal teaching and not emancipated."[27] But the very word emancipation had become equivocal. After the fall of the Girardin enterprise, de Séprès had retitled his journal *Emancipation*, generously plumped up with the best essays by the National Lycée students. A Society for the Propagation of Universal Teaching became associated with it—a society whose vice-president pleaded eloquently for the necessity of qualified masters and the impossibility of fathers of poor families concerning themselves with their children's education. The difference had to be underlined: Jacotot's journal, the one that his two sons edited under his dictation—illness prevented him from writing; he was obliged to hold up a head that no longer wanted to hold itself straight—this journal thus took the title of *Journal de philosophie panécastique*. In its image, the faithful created a Society for Panecastic Philosophy. No one would try to take that name away from him.

We know what it meant: in each intellectual manifestation, there is a totality of human intelligence. The panecastician is a lover of discourse, like the mischievous Socrates and the naïve Phaedrus. But unlike Plato's protagonists, he doesn't recognize any hierarchy among orators or discourses. What interests him is, on the contrary, looking for their equality. He doesn't expect truth from any discourse. Truth is felt and not spoken. It furnishes a rule governing the speaker's conduct, but it will never be manifested in his sentences. Nor does the panecastian judge the morality of a discourse. The morality that counts for him is the one that presides over the act of speaking and writing, that of the intention to communicate, of recognizing the other as an intellectual subject capable of understanding what another intellectual subject wants to say to him. The panecastician is interested in all discourses, in every intellectual manifestation, to a unique end: to verify that they put the same intelligence to work, to verify, by translating the one into the other, the equality of intelligence.

This presupposed an original relation to the debates of the time. The intellectual battle on the subject of the people and its capacity was raging: de Lamennais had published his *Book of the People*. Jean Louis Lerminier, a repentant Saint-Simonian and oracle of the *Revue des deux mondes*, had denounced the book's inconsistency. George Sand, in her turn, had raised the flag of the people and its sovereignty. The *Journal de philosophie panécastique* analyzed each of these intellectual manifestations. Each pretended to attest to the truth of a political camp. That was something that concerned the citizen, but the panecastician got nothing out of it. What interested him in that cascade of refutations was the art that some used to express what they meant. He would show how, by translating themselves to each other, they were translating a thousand other poems, a thousand other adventures of the human mind, of classical works from the story of Bluebeard to the retorts of proletarians on the Place Maubert.

The search for art was not a learned person's pleasure. It was a philosophy, the only one the people could practice. The old philosophies *said* the truth and taught morals. They supposed, for that, a high degree of learning. The panecastician, on the other hand, didn't say the truth and preached no morals. And it was simple and easy, like the story each person tells of his intellectual adventures. "It's the story of each one of us. . . . No matter what your specialty is, shepherd or king, you can discuss the human mind. Intelligence is at work in all trades; it is seen at all the levels of the social ladder. . . . The father and the son, both ignorant, can talk to each other about panecastics."[28]

The problem of the proletarians, excluded from the official society and from political representation, was no different from the problem of the learned and the powerful: like them, they couldn't become men in the full sense of the word except by *recognizing* equality. Equality is not given, nor is it claimed; it is practiced, it is *verified*. And proletarians couldn't verify it except by recognizing the equality of intelligence of their champions and their adversaries. They were undoubtedly interested, for example, in freedom of the press, under attack from the September 1835 laws. But they had to recognize that the reasoning of the defenders of that principle had neither more nor less force in trying to establish it than its adversaries had trying to refute it. In short, said some, I want people to have the liberty to say everything they should have the liberty to say. In short, responded the others, I don't want people to have the liberty to say everything they shouldn't have the liberty to say. What was important—the manifestation of liberty—lay elsewhere: in the equal *art* that, in order to support these antagonistic positions, the one translated from the other; in the *esteem* for that power of the intelligence that doesn't cease being exercised at the very heart of rhetorical irrationality; in the *recognition* of what speaking can mean for whoever renounces the pretension of being right and saying the truth at the price of the other's death. To appropriate for oneself that art, to conquer that reason—this was what counted for the proletarians. One must first be a man before being a citizen. "Whatever side in this fight he might take as a citizen, as a panecastician he must admire his adversaries' minds. A proletarian, rejected by the class of electors, is not required to find equitable what he regards as a usurpation or to like usurpers. But he must study the art of those who explain to him how he is plundered for his own good."[29]

There was nothing else to do but to persist in indicating the extravagant path that consists in seizing in every sentence, in every act, the *side of equality*. Equality was not an end to attain, but a point of departure, a *supposition* to maintain in every circumstance. Never would truth speak up for it. Never would equality exist except in its verification and at the price of being verified always and everywhere. This was not a speech to be made to the people; it was only an example, or rather a few examples, to point out while conversing. It was a moral of the *failure* and the *distance* to be held to the end with whoever wanted to share it:

Seek the truth and you will not find it, knock at its door and it will not open to you, but that *search* will serve you in learning to do. . . . Stop drinking at that fountain, but don't, for all that, stop trying to drink. . . . Come and we will make our poetry. Long live the panecastic philosophy! It's a storyteller who never runs out of stories. It gives itself over to the pleasure of the imagination without having to settle accounts with the truth. It sees that veiled figure only beneath the travesties that hide it. It is content to see those masks, to analyze them, without being tormented by the countenance underneath. The Old Master is never content. He lifts up a mask, rejoices, but his joy doesn't last long; he soon perceives that the mask he has taken off covers another one, and so on until the end of all truth-seekers. The lifting of those superimposed masks is what we call the history of philosophy. Oh! the beautiful history! I like the panecastic stories better.[30]

Emancipation's Tomb

And so ends the *Mélanges posthumes de philosophie panécastique*, published in 1841 by Joseph Jacotot's sons, Victor, the doctor, and Fortuné, the lawyer. The Founder died on August 7, 1840. On his tomb in the Père-Lachaise cemetery, the disciples inscribed the credo of intellectual emancipation: I BELIEVE THAT GOD CREATED THE HUMAN SOUL CAPABLE OF TEACHING ITSELF BY ITSELF, AND WITHOUT A MASTER. This kind of thing is certainly not written, even on the marble of a tomb. A few months later, the inscription was desecrated.

The news of the desecration appeared in the *Journal de l'émancipation intellectuelle*, whose flame Victor and Fortuné Jacotot tried to keep alive. But one cannot replace the voice of a solitary man, even when one has, for many years, held his pen. From issue to issue, the *Journal* filled up with the expanding accounts that Devaureix, an attorney at the Lyon court, made of the activities of the Institute of the Word Incarnate that Louis Guillard, it will be recalled, ran in Lyon according to the principles he learned on his trip to Louvain: teaching should be founded on the maxim "Know yourself." Thus the daily self-examination practiced by the young souls of the pensioners gave them the moral force that presided over their intellectual apprenticeships.

In the September 1842 issue, the hard and pure panecasticians protested this curious application of the emancipatory doctrine. But it was no longer the moment for debate. Two months later, the *Journal de l'émancipation intellectuelle* in its turn fell silent.

The Founder had predicted it all: universal teaching wouldn't take. He had also added that it would not perish.

Notes

Notes

The place of publication on French-language works is Paris unless otherwise noted.

Translator's Introduction

1. Jacques Rancière (with Alain Faure), *La Parole ouvrière* (1976); Rancière, *La Nuit des prolétaires* (1981), translated by Donald Reid as *The Nights of Labor* (Philadelphia, 1989); Rancière, *Le Philosophe plébéien*, ed. Louis Gabriel Gauny (1983).
2. *Révoltes logiques* collective, *L'Empire du sociologue* (1984), p. 7.
3. All three works have been translated into English by Richard Nice: *The Inheritors* (Chicago, 1979); *Reproduction* (London, 1977); *Distinction* (Cambridge, Mass., 1985).
4. *L'Empire du sociologue*, p. 7.
5. Jacques Rancière, "L'Ethique de la sociologie," in ibid., p. 28.
6. Ibid., pp. 28, 29.
7. Jacques Rancière, review of J.-C. Milner, *De l'école, La Quinzaine littéraire*, 422 (Aug. 1984).
8. Louis Althusser, "Problèmes étudiants," *La Nouvelle Critique*, 152 (Jan. 1964).
9. Louis Althusser's "Ideology and Ideological State Apparatuses" appeared originally in *La Pensée* in 1970. It was translated the following year in *Lenin and Philosophy*, tr. Ben Brewster (New York, 1971), pp. 127–86.
10. *La Leçon d'Althusser* (1974), p. 35.
11. Jacques Rancière interview with François Ewald, "Qu'est-ce que la classe ouvrière?," *Magazine littéraire*, 175 (July–Aug. 1981).

12. See, in particular, Jacques Rancière, *Le Philosophe et ses pauvres* (1983).

13. See Jacques Rancière, *Aux bords du politique* (1990).

14. Walter Benjamin, "Theses on the Philosophy of History," in *Illuminations*, ed. Hannah Arendt (New York, 1969).

15. *Révoltes logiques* collective, "Deux ou trois choses que l'historien ne veut pas savoir," *Le Mouvement social*, 100 (July–Sept. 1977).

16. Bourdieu, *Reproduction*, p. iv.

Chapter One

1. Félix and Victor Ratier, "Enseignement universel: Emancipation intellectuelle," *Journal de philosophie panécastique*, 5 (1838): 155.

2. J. S. Van de Weyer, *Sommaire des leçons publiques de M. Jacotot sur les principes de l'enseignement universel* (Brussels, 1822), p. 11.

3. J. Jacotot, *Enseignement universel: Langue maternelle*, 6th ed. (1836), p. 448; *Journal de l'émancipation intellectuelle*, 3 (1835–36): 121.

4. J. Jacotot, *Enseignement universel: Langue étrangère*, 2d ed. (1829), p. 219.

Chapter Two

1. J. Jacotot, *Enseignement universel: Mathématiques*, 2d ed. (1829), pp. 50–51.

2. *Lettre du Fondateur de l'enseignement universel au général Lafayette* (Louvain, 1829), p. 6.

3. *Journal de l'émancipation intellectuelle*, 3 (1835–36): 15.

4. Ibid., p. 380.

5. B. Gonod, *Nouvelle exposition de la méthode de Joseph Jacotot* (1830), pp. 12–13.

6. J. Jacotot, *Enseignement universel: Langue maternelle*, 6th ed. (1836), pp. 464–65.

7. *Journal de l'émancipation intellectuelle*, 3 (1835–36): 9.

8. Ibid., p. 11.   9. Ibid., 6 (1841–42): 72.

10. Ibid., p. 73.   11. Ibid.

12. C. Lorain, *Réfutation de la méthode Jacotot* (1830), p. 90.

13. Jacotot, *Langue maternelle*, p. 271; *Journal de l'émancipation intellectuelle*, 3 (1835–36): 323.

14. *Journal de l'émancipation intellectuelle*, 3 (1835–36): 253.

15. Ibid., p. 259.
16. Ibid., 4 (1836–37): 280.
17. Jacotot, *Langue maternelle*, p. 422.
18. A. Destutt de Tracy, *Observations sur le système actuel d'instruction publique* (Year IX).
19. J. S. Van de Weyer, *Sommaire des leçons publiques de M. Jacotot sur les principes de l'enseignement universel* (Brussels, 1822), p. 23.
20. Plato, *Cratylus*, 399c: "Alone among the animals, man was called *anthropos* precisely because he examines what he sees (*anathron ha opope*)."
21. J. Jacotot, *Enseignement universel: Musique*, 3d ed. (1830), p. 349.
22. See Plato, *Phaedrus*, 274c/277a; and Jacques Rancière, *Le Philosophe et ses pauvres* (1983), especially p. 66.
23. *Journal de l'émancipation intellectuelle*, 5 (1838): 168.
24. J. Jacotot, *Mélanges posthumes de philosophie panécastique* (1841), p. 176.
25. *Journal de l'émancipation intellectuelle*, 3 (1835–36): 334.
26. B. Froussard, *Lettre à ses amis au sujet de la méthode de M. Jacotot* (1829), p. 6.

Chapter Three

1. J. Jacotot, *Enseignement universel: Langue étrangère*, 2d ed. (1829), pp. 228–29.
2. Ibid., p. 229.
3. J. Jacotot, *Enseignement universel: Langue maternelle*, 6th ed. (1836), p. 199.
4. L. de Bonald, *Recherches philosophiques sur les premiers objets des connaissances morales* (1818), vol. 1, p. 67.
5. L. de Bonald, *Legislation primitive considérée dans les premiers temps par les seules lumières de la raison*, in *Oeuvres complètes* (1859), vol. 1, p. 1161; de Bonald, *Recherches philosophiques*, vol. 1, p. 105.
6. M. Maine de Biran, "Les Recherches philosophiques de M. de Bonald," in *Oeuvres complètes* (1939), vol. 12, p. 252.
7. *Journal de l'émancipation intellectuelle*, 4 (1836–37): 430–31.
8. J. Jacotot, *Enseignement universel: Droit et philosophie panécastique* (1838), p. 278.
9. Jacotot, *Langue maternelle*, p. 330.
10. Ibid., p. 33.

11. *Journal de l'émancipation intellectuelle*, 4 (1836–37): 187.
12. Jacotot, *Droit et philosophie panécastique*, p. 42.
13. Ibid., p. 41.
14. *L'Observateur belge*, 16, 426 (1818): 142–43.
15. Jacotot, *Droit et philosophie panécastique*, pp. 11–13.
16. Ibid., p. 231.
17. J. Jacotot, *Enseignement universel: Musique*, 3d ed. (1830), p. 163.
18. Ibid., p. 314.
19. Jacotot, *Droit et philosophie panécastique*, p. 91.
20. Jacotot, *Musique*, p. 347.
21. Jacotot, *Langue maternelle*, p. 149.
22. Jacotot, *Musique*, p. 322.
23. Jacotot, *Langue maternelle*, p. 281.
24. Ibid., p. 284.   25. Ibid., p. 282.
26. Ibid., p. 243.   27. Jacotot, *Musique*, p. 338.
28. *Journal de philosophie panécastique*, 5 (1838): 265.

Chapter Four

1. F. J. Dumbeck, *Annales Academiae Lovaniensis*, 9 (1825–26): 216, 220, 222.
2. *Journal de l'émancipation intellectuelle*, 3 (1835–36): 223.
3. J. Jacotot, *Mélanges posthumes de philosophie panécastique* (1841), p. 118.
4. J. Jacotot, *Enseignement universel: Langue étrangère*, 2d ed. (1829), p. 75.
5. Jacotot, *Mélanges posthumes*, p. 116.
6. J. Jacotot, *Enseignement universel: Musique*, 3d ed. (1830), p. 52.
7. J. Jacotot, *Enseignement universel: Langue maternelle*, 6th ed. (1836), p. 278.
8. Ibid., p. 91.
9. Ibid., pp. 362–63.
10. "If one points out a vice in our institutions and proposes a remedy for it, immediately a great functionary stands up and, without discussing the proposition, cries out in a serious manner: 'I'm not prepared to examine the question, I admit my incapacity, etc.' But here is the hidden meaning of his words: 'If a man like me, highly situated and gifted with genius proportionate to his dignity, admits his inability, isn't it presumptuous, isn't it madness on the part of

those who pretend to have a ready-made opinion?' This is an indirect method of intimidation; it's arrogance beneath a very thin veil of modesty." Jeremy Bentham, *Traité des sophismes parlementaires*, tr. Etienne Dumont (Paris, 1840), p. 84.

11. E. Dumont, preface to Jeremy Bentham, *Tactique des assemblées parlementaires* (Geneva, 1816), p. xv.

12. Jeremy Bentham, "Essay on Political Tactics," in vol. 2 of *The Works of Jeremy Bentham*, ed. John Bowring (New York, 1926), p. 306.

13. Jacotot, *Langue maternelle*, pp. 328–29.

14. *Journal de l'émancipation intellectuelle*, 4 (1836–37): 357.

15. Jacotot, *Langue maternelle*, p. 339.

16. Ibid., p. 109.

17. Jacotot, *Musique*, pp. 194–95.

18. Ibid., p. 195.

19. Jacotot, *Langue maternelle*, p. 365.

20. J. Jacotot, "Le Contrat social," in *Journal de philosophie panécastique*, 5 (1838): 62.

21. Ibid., p. 211.

22. Jacotot, *Langue étrangère*, p. 123.

23. Jacotot, *Langue maternelle*, pp. 289–90.

24. Ibid., p. 359.   25. Ibid., p. 356.

26. Ibid., p. 342.   27. Plato, *Phaedrus*, 273e.

28. P.-S. Ballanche, "Essais de palingénésie sociale: Formule générale de l'histoire de tous les peuples appliquée à l'histoire du peuple romain," *Revue de Paris*, April 1829: 155.

29. J. Jacotot, *Manuel de l'émancipation intellectuelle* (1841), p. 15.

Chapter Five

1. P. Reter de Brigton, *Manuel populaire de la méthode Jacotot* (1830), p. 3.

2. J. Jacotot, *Enseignement universel: Mathématiques*, 2d ed. (1829), p. 97.

3. Ibid., pp. 1–2.

4. *Journal de philosophie panécastique*, 5 (1838): 1–12.

5. Ibid., p. 277.

6. Ibid., p. 279.

7. J. de Lasteyrie, *Résumé de la méthode de l'enseignement universel d'après M. Jacotot* (1829), pp. xxvii–xxviii.

8. J. Jacotot, *Enseignement universel: Langue maternelle*, 6th ed. (1836), pp. 446, 448.

9. See *Remarques sur la méthode de M. Jacotot* (Brussels, 1827); and *L'Université protégée par l'ânerie des disciples de Joseph Jacotot* (1830).

10. *Journal d'éducation et d'instruction*, 4: 81–83, 264–66.

11. *Journal de l'émancipation intellectuelle*, 4 (1836–37): 328.

12. Jacotot, *Mathématiques*, pp. 21–22.

13. Ibid., p. 143.

14. Ibid., p. 22.

15. Ibid., p. 21.

16. *Journal de philosophie panécastique*, 5 (1838): 279.

17. *Journal des connaissances utiles*, 3 (1833): 63.

18. Ibid., 2, 2 (Feb. 1832): 19–21.

19. Ibid., 3: 208–10.

20. *Journal de l'émancipation intellectuelle*, 4 (1836–37): 328.

21. Jacotot, *Mathématiques*, pp. 191–92.

22. J. Jacotot, *Enseignement universel: Droit et philosophie panécastique* (1838), p. 342.

23. Ibid., pp. 330–31.

24. F. de Lamennais, *Le Livre du peuple* (1838), p. 65, cited in *Journal de la philosophie panécastique*, 5 (1838): 144.

25. A paraphrase of de Lamennais, *Livre du peuple*, p. 73, in ibid., p. 145.

26. Jacotot, *Mathématiques*, p. 22.

27. *Journal de l'émancipation intellectuelle*, 3 (1835–36): 276.

28. Jacotot, *Droit et philosophie panécastique*, p. 214.

29. Ibid., p. 293.

30. J. Jacotot, *Mélanges posthumes de philosophie panécastique* (1841), pp. 349–51.

CPSIA information can be obtained
at www.ICGtesting.com
Printed in the USA
LVOW08s1115080917
547971LV00001B/1/P